SONOS
The Home Sound System

Listen Better
at sonos.com

The scandinavian watch brand that's resetting the standard for women's watches

Shop the SS17 collection

at mockberg.com

A Mockberg watch is more than a way to keep track of time: It's a sophisticated and classic accent that's just as comfortable in the great outdoors as it is at a glamorous fashion event. The watches are designed from light materials of great quality to let you move about your day with ease. Whether you are running to a meeting, walking outdoors or attending a glamorous fashion event; the Mockberg watch will be there, resting on your wrist. With a stainless steel case and genuine leather strap, the Mockberg watch weighs only 30 grams which means that you barely notice that you are wearing it.

aiaλu

AIAYU IS MADE TO LAST

St. Strandstræde 12 A, Copenhagen
aiayu.com

AIAYU STORE IN THE MAKING

OPENING MARCH 2017
COPENHAGEN

Signed, Sealed, Delivered.

Featuring 12 new images, The Balance Edition of the Kinfolk Notecard Collection
is available now on Kinfolk.com and in selected stores.

Unique wooden floors since 1898

KINFOLK

EDITOR-IN-CHIEF
Nathan Williams

EDITOR
Julie Cirelli

CREATIVE DIRECTOR
Anja Charbonneau

DEPUTY EDITOR
John Clifford Burns

DESIGN DIRECTOR
Alex Hunting

ASSISTANT EDITOR
Molly Mandell

COPY EDITOR
Rachel Holzman

PROOFREADER
Kelsey Burrow

WEB ADMINISTRATOR
Jesse Hiestand

COMMUNICATIONS DIRECTOR
Jessica Gray

ADVERTISING DIRECTOR
Pamela Mullinger

PUBLISHING DIRECTOR
Amy Woodroffe

SALES & DISTRIBUTION DIRECTOR
Frédéric Mähl

CASTING DIRECTOR
Sarah Bunter

ACCOUNTING MANAGER
Paige Bischoff

WEB EDITOR
Nikolaj Hansson

MANAGING DIRECTOR
Doug Bischoff

OUUR DESIGNER
Mario Depicolzuane

OUUR COLLECTION DESIGNER
Hanna Rauhala

STUDIO MANAGER
Monique Schröder

EDITORIAL ASSISTANTS
Lucrezia Biasutti
Ulrika Lukševica

DESIGN ASSISTANTS
Benja Pavlin
Océane Torti

OPERATIONS ASSISTANTS
Margriet Kalsbeek

CONTRIBUTING EDITORS
Michael Anastassiades
Jonas Bjerre-Poulsen
Ilse Crawford
Frida Escobedo
Rose Forde
Margot Henderson
Leonard Koren
Hans Ulrich Obrist
Amy Sall
Matt Willey

ILLUSTRATION
Frédéric Forest
Chidy Wayne

STYLING & SET DESIGN
Yolande Gagnier
Lilja Hrönn Helgadóttir
Debbie Hsieh
Sam Jaspersohn
Anna Klein
Sandy Suffield
Alpha Vomero

WORDS
Alex Anderson
John Clifford Burns
River Clegg
Erin Dixon
Rachel Gallaher
Djassi DaCosta Johnson
Jared Killeen
Harriet Fitch Little
Molly Mandell
Sarah Moroz
Tom Morris
David Plaisant
Debika Ray
Asher Ross
Tristan Rutherford
Charles Shafaieh
Patricia Meyer Spacks
Pip Usher
Molly Young

PHOTOGRAPHY
Christopher Ferguson
Simone Fiorini
Lasse Fløde
Stefan Heinrichs
Julia Hetta
Ken Heyman
Kenneth Josephson
Paul Laib
Pelle Lannefors
LippZahnschirm
Joss McKinley
Jack Mitchell
Mikkel Mortensen
Paola Pansini
Marc Riboud
Danilo Scarpati
Philippe Servent
Robert Severi
Marsý Hild Þórsdóttir
Aaron Tilley
Zoltan Tombor
Abisag Tüllmann
Adam Wiseman

ISSUE 23

info@kinfolk.com
www.kinfolk.com

Published by Ouur Media
Amagertorv 14, Level 1
1160 Copenhagen, Denmark

The views expressed in Kinfolk magazine are those of the respective contributors and are not necessarily shared by the company or its staff.

SUBSCRIBE
Kinfolk is published four times a year. To subscribe, visit kinfolk.com/subscribe or email us at info@kinfolk.com

CONTACT US
If you have questions or comments, please write to us at info@kinfolk.com. For advertising inquiries, get in touch at advertising@kinfolk.com

Publication Design
by Alex Hunting

Printed in Canada
by Hemlock Printers Ltd.

LEVI'S®
MADE & CRAFTED®

ARTFUL CONSTRUCTION. ELEVATED DETAILS.
LEVI'S® BY DESIGN.

"The only way forward is the less-but-better way: back to simplicity."
DIETER RAMS — P. 112

Photograph: Adam Wiseman

"Take a navigation system with you if you must, but it is better to experience uncertainty."
TIPS — P.148

Photograph: Marsý Hild Þórsdóttir

NORSE PROJECTS

Issue 23

Welcome

Of all the states of human consciousness, there are none that throw the passage of time into such brilliant relief as sleep. A little-understood physical phenomenon often characterized as "an altered state of human consciousness"—that slippery psychological catch-all that also includes euphoria, psychedelic drug use, meditation, hypnosis and prayer—sleep and its rituals have captured the human imagination in art and literature for centuries. Proust described it as the vestigial measure of time passing. "When a man is asleep, he has in a circle round him the chain of the hours, the sequence of the years, the order of the heavenly host," he famously wrote in *Swann's Way*. "Instinctively, he consults them when he awakes, and in an instant reads off his own position on the earth's surface and the time that has elapsed during his slumbers."

We explore the various theories of sleep in this issue of *Kinfolk*, along with other elements of perception, like color, reality and beauty. Why do so many people find the sound of meandering, repetitive stories soothing? And why are specific colors so difficult to remember?

On page 62, Harriet Fitch Little navigates conflicting advice on the best way to sleep, and on page 38, Pip Usher examines the psychological connection between memory and color. In a rare interview, industrial design icon Dieter Rams ruminates on his singular quest for simplicity, admitting that it is deceptively hard to achieve. Elsewhere in our Features section, we examine the adversity-defying history of Dance Theatre of Harlem, and British actor Elisa Lasowski makes a case for establishing a personal trajectory in an industry beset by superficial demands.

In our special Weekend section, we join composer Leonard Bernstein on his 1967 vacation, meet design doyenne Rossana Orlandi and receive tips from some of the most interesting weekenders in six cities. We revisit some classic ways to pass the weekend hours, like rereading beloved books and doing laundry. We also give advice on how to embrace ennui: how to do nothing, trust our internal navigation systems to explore, get naked and—importantly in today's world—use our time in a meaningful way to advocate for society's most vulnerable.

NATHAN WILLIAMS & JULIE CIRELLI

SØRENSEN

Art must take reality by surprise.

— Françoise Sagan

Sorensen. Luxury leather for the most
iconic designs in the world

S 19 73

PEAU SØRENSEN LEATHER LÆDER LEDER PIEL

sorensenleather.com

1

Starters

ALEX ANDERSON

Meaningful Coincidence

Is there a difference between chance and coincidence? *Alex Anderson* explores whether happenstance can ever really "just happen."

Leonardo da Vinci could perceive worlds in the stains and markings on old, weathered walls, and he eagerly counseled other painters to study walls so as to shape their own imaginings of landscapes, figures in motion and facial expressions.

His arcane advice struck me recently while I was looking up other things in his notebooks. Not an hour later, I read the same bit of Leonardo's crafty guidance on a friend's Instagram feed posted from 3,000 miles away. Odd. Later that same day, I came across the curious word "metis" twice in quick succession—first on a map and then on a construction sign. Metis is an ancient Greek term often associated with Leonardo da Vinci, connoting wisdom and magical cunning. Leonardo, again: Was I sensing a meaningful pattern?

I was certainly witnessing an instance of the Baader-Meinhof phenomenon. So named by Stanford linguistics professor Arnold Zwicky, it "occurs when a person, after having learned some (usually obscure) fact, word, phrase or other item for the first time, encounters that item again, perhaps several times, shortly after having learned it." The scientific thinker puts this down to a cognitive bias called "frequency illusion," whereby the first awareness of such an item makes the mind especially attentive to other instances of it. What might appear to be meaningful coincidence is instead a shift in attention that allows us to associate unrelated things that otherwise would have passed without notice. A more imaginative disposition finds this explanation limiting and intolerably bland.

Two aspects of the Baader-Meinhof phenomenon bear con-

sideration: the items that keep popping up and the meanings associated with them. In "Exercise in Timing," American poet William Carlos Williams poignantly evokes the significance of one such item: "Oh / the sumac died/ it's/ the first time / I / noticed it." Except for a few weeks each fall when it turns gloriously crimson, sumac is a weedy, unobtrusive inhabitant of shaggy forest borders and desultory gardens. In the poem, though, the plant discloses itself, entangles the events of death and noticing, and provokes a sudden realization of the seemingly insignificant carriers of meaning we encounter around us. I've intentionally referred to the sumac, rather than the poet, as the carrier of meaning, because it so often feels like meaning is discovered, rather than ascribed.

In our interactions with things, words and events—and more particularly in their overlaps and associations—we *find* meaning rather than *give* meaning. Christian Norberg-Schulz, a Norwegian architectural theoretician and author of *Genius Loci* (a title that evokes the ancient Latin reference to the protective spirit of a place), explains that this sort of thinking uncovers "the meanings inherent in the life-world," which are especially dense in certain objects and places. Things, he explains, gather meaning to themselves.

In his book *Synchronicity: An Acausal Connecting Principle*, the pioneering psychologist Carl Jung struggled to explain this notion that meaning is somehow "out there," already attached to things and events. He wanted to show how an intuitive sense of the meaningful world could coexist with the

scientifically verifiable concept of cause and effect, which clearly organizes chains of events, but inadequately explains their significance. "We are so accustomed to regard meaning as a psychic process or content," he protests, "that it never enters our heads to suppose that it could also exist outside the psyche." Synchronicity binds across seemingly unrelated sequences of events with what Jung calls an "inconstant connection through contingence, equivalence, or 'meaning.'" It is this inconstant connection that people who experience the Baader-Meinhof phenomenon suddenly confront. Events they discover to be meaningfully linked are bound, even though they remain parts of otherwise unrelated chains of events.

According to Jung, most cultures would have readily accepted such an idea before the rise of natural science; mindfulness of preternatural connections was acute when a scientific understanding of causality was limited. Our contemporary understanding of cause and effect at every scale has blinded us to other kinds of meaningful connections. But was Leonardo da Vinci off the mark when he saw in the aged stones and stained plaster of the walls around him "diverse combats and figures in quick movement"? Are we wrong to find meaning in the tenuous links between disparate but coincident statements or words? Perhaps when we attune our perception to subtle correlations among things and happenings in the world we are not merely deluded into considering them meaningful; we are discovering the meaning already present in them.

Right: As its name implies, the Piece Round stool by Take Home Design is composed of small pieces of walnut or oak connected in a circular composition.

CHARLES SHAFAIEH

The Power of Influence

How is it that throughout history, similar ideas have often cropped up in different locations and, at times, seemingly simultaneously?

"The history of technology depends little on man and his freedom," Milan Kundera writes in *The Curtain*. "Obedient to its own logic, it cannot be other than what it has been or what it will be . . . If Edison had not invented the light-bulb, someone else would have."

In fact, prior to Thomas Edison, about 20 people were working on similar inventions. And analogous circumstances apply to the origins of calculus, the polio vaccine, the telephone and the theories of evolution and relativity, to name just a few. Kundera's reading of technological development as linear and indifferent to the person behind a discovery rings true. Breakthroughs occur anywhere, it seems, and are only a matter of time.

Whether or not an idea will be widespread or well received can be influenced by the originator of the idea and how they are perceived. But more important than an individual's likability may be both the number of bonds they share with others and, paradoxically, how weak those ties are. Sociologist Mark Granovetter observes that "if one tells a rumor to all his close friends, and they do likewise, many will hear the rumor a second and third time since those linked by strong ties tend to share friends." Conversely, tell mere acquaintances—such as those loosely connected by social media—and the same rumor can spread more widely and with greater speed.

The breadth of an idea's appeal can be difficult to measure, due to the prevalence of what economist Timur Kuran calls "preference falsification," or the difference between one's private and public opinions. Throughout Eastern Europe in 1989 and in many Arab nations in the early 2010s, the magnitude of social unrest shocked the world. People questioned how so many could suddenly break from the status quo. Yet those who had long embraced revolutionary ideals were not surprised; they just needed an impetus, however small, to express their sentiments openly. Such actions reveal that what may look like the spontaneous expression of a new zeitgeist is often anything but.

BRIGHT IDEA
by Molly Mandell

Brass light fixtures first gained popularity in the Victorian era, reappearing during the Edwardian era, the modernist '30s and again among the *Mad Men*-style interiors of the '60s. Today, brass is back in the proverbial spotlight. The placement of lighting can have a dramatic effect on the ambience of a room, so Kalmar Werkstätten designed its Hase table lamp (top) with a leather grip for easy repositioning. The Helios lamp (center) by American design studio Workstead functions as both a light source and an objet d'art. Lastly, architect David Chipperfield reinterpreted the classic desk light to create the Chipperfield w102 lamp (bottom) in collaboration with Wästberg.

Left photograph: Aaron Tilley, Set Design: Sandy Suffield. Right photographs: Mikkel Mortensen

Photograph: Marsý Hild Þórsdóttir, Styling: Lilja Hrönn Helgadóttir, Hair & Makeup: Carly Lim

ERIN DIXON

Pernilla Ohrstedt

Wrestling with ideas about a rapidly urbanizing future, an emerging architect makes an optimistic case for doing more with less.

Through intuitive, interactive spaces and communicative objects, London-based Swedish architect Pernilla Ohrstedt exploits the field's inherent complexity. Her work challenges perceptions, reshapes the present and imagines a beautiful future in which technology helps create a smarter, more agile and compassionate world.

Beyond the words of "architecture" and "design," how do you describe what you do? I like to describe what I do as "designing performances"—performances between spaces and people, objects and people, and objects and buildings. I'm always interested in the interaction between things.

Is there an overarching philosophy that guides your work? There are a number of things that are really important to me. I see architecture as a way of empowering people. It's about making people comfortable, making them explore and making them brave. I think that the places in which we exist form us.

It's also about creating things from minimal means. With a lot of money you can do a lot of things, but being resourceful is crucial. You have to ask yourself: Why am I making something? One thing we quote to our students at the Architectural Association School of Architecture is from Cedric Price: "No one should be interested in the design of bridges. They should be concerned with how to get to the other side." That's a really important ambition: Not to build just to build, but to consider why you are building something in the first place.

Is your vision of the future pessimistic or optimistic? It's definitely optimistic. Of course, there are lots of troubling things going on, but one of the things we know is how little we know about the future. We just understand that it's developing at a very, very high speed. We can't foresee where technology will take us, but we know that in 15 years, there will be a shift that we can't conceive of now. I feel incredibly fortunate to be living through this global era, an era in which we can take advantage of knowledge, cultures and insight from around the world. I hope that that continues. It's fundamentally positive and empowering, and brings with it positive outcomes.

HARRIET FITCH LITTLE

Careless Whisper

Turn on, tune in, zone out: The pleasures and phenomena of half listening.

"A pleasurable headache." "A bristling feeling as if a bug flew past my ear." "That tickly feeling you get in your stomach when you drive over hills."

Since the term Autonomous Sensory Meridian Response (ASMR) was coined six years ago, millions of devotees have struggled to describe the satisfaction they experience when listening to certain types of soothing sounds and voices.

There is an online industry that caters to coaxing these tingles—so-called ASMRtists (a full-time job for the most popular) who record videos of themselves performing pretend eye exams in hushed tones, explaining how to fold towels, or going through the contents of their make-up box and slowly tapping all the brushes. These are the simple, repetitive tasks that enthusiasts say send shivers of pleasure running through them.

What is ASMR? For medical professionals, it lingers in the realm of pseudoscience. It's an internet phenomenon whose reputation is not helped by its peculiar name ("meridian" is borrowed from traditional Chinese medicine) and the propensity of its exponents to spout shaky theories of oxytocin, pleasure receptors and even seizures to explain what they experience.

But skeptics would do well curb their incredulity. While it is true that the internet has facilitated the formation of communities around every niche interest imaginable, there is nothing new about the notion that there is relaxation—even pleasure—to be gleaned from listening to sounds that follow no discernable pattern, particularly if those sounds are human.

Think, for example, of Dylan Thomas' celebrated 1954 radio play *Under Milk Wood*. Thomas takes as his subject matter the mad inhabitants of a small Welsh village, whose lives he describes with little sense of plot or even logic— "drunk with melody" as the critic Robert Graves described it.

Without a storyline to follow, listening to Thomas' play becomes a gentle, meditative experience— the "sloeblack, slow, black, crow-black, fishingboat-bobbing sea" a lullaby that can send tingles down the spine of even the most cynical.

Often, the effect is accidental. The BBC shipping forecast has secured the status of national treasure in the UK despite the fact that no one except seafarers understands its coded announcements—"Tyne, Dogger. Northeast 3 or 4. Occasional rain. Moderate or poor..." Peter Jefferson, who read the shipping forecast for 40 years and regularly receives fan mail from listeners who used it as a sleep aid, had a hypothesis as to its popularity: "The sound of another human voice, familiar yet not intrusive, reciting this mantra, can be quite relaxing."

Increasingly, and inevitably, people have found ways to monetize the effect. Sound therapy works by immersing clients in "sound baths" that the therapist creates with bells and whispered words. Practitioners describe it as akin to meditation, but rather than actively emptying one's mind—a task that many find impossible—the racing brain is distracted by inconsequential noises, achieving a similar effect.

In truth, there is no need to pay for the experience. ASMR is one option, and for those who find the videos strange, podcasts offer an expanding universe of alternatives. *Under Milk Wood* finds its contemporary counterpart in absurdist audio dramas such as *Welcome to Night Vale*—a mock community radio broadcast in which hypnotizing glow clouds and floating cats are reported on in calm, reassuring tones. Despite the fact it is hard to follow a plot between episodes, the show is one of the most popular podcasts on iTunes and has spawned a host of imitators.

Other podcasts embrace the calming effect of voices more explicitly. It is telling that the most popular bedtime podcast, *Sleep With Me*, offers no direct encouragements to fall asleep. Instead, host Drew Ackerman boasts that he will "bore you to sleep" with his meandering, repetitive stories.

Perhaps the voices can make you tingle. If they do, rest assured you are not the impressionable victim of a modern fad—Virginia Woolf described what would now be called ASMR in *Mrs. Dalloway*. She wrote of a whisper that "rasped his spine deliciously and sent running up into his brain waves of sound which, concussing, broke."

The lore of La Pitchoune, the fabled French summerhouse of *Julia Child.*

Julia Child had a knack for wonderful homes: be it her charmed upbringing in Pasadena or in the Edenic beauty of Ceylon (now Sri Lanka), where she served as an intelligence officer in World War II; in Sichuan Province; Bonn; Oslo or Cambridge. And, of course, there's her beloved apartment in the 7th Arrondissement of Paris that she stuffed to the gills with pots and pans, and where she first began work on the book that made her an American icon.

But she loved no place so well as La Pitchoune (or "La Peetch" as she preferred it), the modest stucco house that she and her husband, Paul, built in Provence, France. La Peetch was the apotheosis of Child's love for France. She called it her "spiritual home" and for nearly three decades would retreat there to decompress, edit her work and luxuriate with Paul. But most of all, it was where she cooked, relentlessly testing her recipes and throwing long dinner parties. James Beard and M.F.K. Fisher were habitués; dinner guests included Robert Penn Warren, Max Ernst and Sybille Bedford. Everything, we can hear Child say in her peerless warble, was "absolutely *delicious!*"

The red-tile roof, the lavender and mimosa, the olive trees brimming with fruit, the winding hillscape that rose behind the house into volcanic mountains, the local provisioners, the dusty driveway that could barely accommodate her Citroën—these were romances for Child. The kitchen at La Peetch, however, was nothing but practical. More efficient than her kitchen in Massachusetts, more heart-and-bones than the faux-windowed set of *The French Chef,* its centerpiece was an enormous pegboard that seemed to hold every pan, whisk and measuring tool that had ever been for sale at Paris' renowned cookware shop, E. Dehillerin. Paul had lovingly outlined each item with a marker, so that it could easily be put back in its place.

There was the large central island, over which Child leaned and sweated, striving to find a basic recipe for baguettes that could be recreated in American kitchens (it took "284 pounds of flour"). And the stove, from which sprang all that is good in life: poulet rôti, sole meunière, lamb en croûte, boudin blanc, bouillabaisse, tarte au citron…

Child made her last visit to La Peetch in 1992. Reliably unsentimental, she had no interest in clinging to the place once Paul became too ill to travel. On the last day in her kitchen at La Peetch, she prepared bœuf en daube à la provençale and thought of new beginnings. She was 80.

ASHER ROSS

La Pitchoune

Photographer Marc Riboud captured Child in her kitchen at La Pitchoune in 1969 while on assignment for Vogue. She would later recall him as being "a small, twinkle-eyed 40-year-old Frenchman."

Photograph: Marc Riboud / Magnum Photos / POLFOTO

CONSCIOUSLY   ARTFULLY   ELEGANTLY

COCLICO

EST MM

THE HOURGLASS

by Charles Shafaieh

When we trace back the origins of the hourglass, we can't find conclusive evidence of its existence before the 14th century. Now 700 years later, we're familiar with seeing sand inside hourglasses, but over the centuries, they've also been filled with powdered marble and crushed eggshells. They first found importance aboard ships as aids in measuring distances traveled—an improvement over millennia-old *clepsydras*, or water clocks. The water clocks could be compromised more easily, even by the condensation produced on humid days. On land, however, use of the hourglass was often more symbolic than functional. While the mechanical clock (invented around the same time) and its intricate inner mechanisms prompted comparison to the movements of the heavenly spheres, the hourglass measured a set period. Its visual staging of time's "end" with each turn could serve as a reminder of mortality. A favorite of artists as a memento mori, it is frequently portrayed in the figurative hands of Death, as in Albrecht Dürer's haunting 16th-century engraving *Knight, Death and the Devil*. In an intriguing twist, some evolutionary biologists argue that women with "hourglass" figures may have higher levels of the reproductive hormone estradiol. So the constricting and oppressive Victorian corset—which forces the female body into an hourglass shape—makes for a deep and poetic irony: In signifying life-giving potential, an often over-fetishized figure embodies a centuries-old symbol of death. *Photography by Aaron Tilley & Set Design by Sandy Suffield*

JOHN CLIFFORD BURNS

Jones

On the road to revelation and the release of a debut album, a British musician offers advice on how to harness massive ambition: Do not yield to self-doubt.

To sing is to make one's voice heard. For singer-songwriter Cherie Jones-Mattis, performing also means broadcasting her inner voice. And that's no mean feat for a woman who prides herself on introspection. Yet despite her shyness and default setting of British reserve, Jones-Mattis' complete commitment to music and burning ambition to be the strongest version of herself has carried her into a profession she's dreamed about since childhood. Shortly after the release of her debut album, *New Skin*, she talks to us about quashing some roadblocks she encountered along the way.

Do you remember the first song that you ever wrote? It was called "I Wish" and I wrote it when I was 15. It was about unrequited love and was definitely a starting point, let's put it that way.

How did you figure out where to go from there? I used to watch a lot of interviews with artistic people and was always curious about their mindset. I discovered that it was mostly about your attitude. You have to have that strong sense of belief in what you're doing, and you have to keep going.

What type of challenges have you faced along the way? The biggest challenge has been self-doubt. Everyone has a little voice in their head that's sometimes nice and sometimes not that nice and can make them second-guess their decisions or talents. Part of my personal journey has been trying to switch that off, or at least tell myself something positive instead. I think that everything in life is a battle with yourself.

How do you feel you've progressed as a musician? If you're ambitious, or if you have some sort of vision, you have to be tough on yourself and keep thinking about what comes next. I'm a bit of a perfectionist, so I'm always trying to improve myself and get better and stronger. At the same time, you have to enjoy where you are and not place your happiness on something that's ahead of you. It's a balance.

Has your perception of the music industry changed since entering it? It's changed a lot. When I was trying to get into it as a teenager, we didn't have social media. I had no idea that when I got to this point, I would have to share so much more of myself. Back then, people just got interviewed about the music, but now you have to share your thoughts and what you're up to on social media.

Does that come naturally to you? Not necessarily. I've always been an introvert, which I've come to love about myself and see as a strength. I understand myself better now. I know that I'm just processing things in a different way than other people. It's strange: You'd think that, being an introvert, I wouldn't be able to perform.

How does it feel, then, to perform in front of an audience? It's very empowering and liberating. It's a special feeling when you look into people's eyes and connect with them. It's one of my favorite things to do.

Where does the sentiment in your songs come from? I get ideas when I'm walking around or late at night that I like to use when I'm going into a writing session. I'm always writing things down on my phone—I have a constant stream of notes. Writing can be very therapeutic when I am going through something—to get my ideas out.

RIVER CLEGG

On Schadenfreude

Do other people make us laugh, or are we laughing at other people? A comedian offers advice on where to draw the line.

Sorry, but I'm afraid this is one of those articles that starts off with a quote by a famous person. Here it is: "Tragedy is when I cut my finger. Comedy is when you fall into an open sewer and die."

Mel Brooks said that, and I think we immediately understand where he's coming from. The misfortune of others has been part of comedy forever. It's like that expression: *comedy equals tragedy plus time.*

The idea is that laughter comes when there's enough distance between you and a Bad Thing for it not to seem like a threat—either because it happened long ago, or because it happened to somebody else, or both.

But does Brooks' quote hold up? Let's look at some classic jokes and see. An obvious one is the Three Stooges' entire oeuvre, in which the guys thumped, slapped and knocked each other into comedy history. That's not to say that violence is the *only* reason their act has endured—we can't discount those great high-pitched squeals, for example—but the infliction of pain played a vital role.

And then there's one of my favorites: Gary Larson's immortal *The Far Side* cartoon series, which statistics suggest is sitting in your office as a daily calendar at this very moment. Larson's work is influential for its economy, its absurdity, and its earthy, dismal take on

middle-American life. But what a lot of people don't recognize about *The Far Side* is that somebody is often in imminent mortal danger.

Take the one with two deer talking to each other in the woods. One has a red bulls-eye on his chest. The other deer says, "Bummer of a birthmark, Hal." Sure, it's funny, but the whole subtext here is that Hal is probably going to die very soon. Then there's one where a rescue pilot is flying over a man stranded on a desert island with the word "HELF" written in the sand. Since it doesn't say "HELP," the pilot cancels the rescue, leaving the guy to starve.

There are plenty of variations on this traditional equation of *Bad Thing + Happening to Somebody Else = Funny.* For example, the snobs-versus-slobs dynamic of movies like *Animal House* and *Caddyshack* arguably makes it even easier to laugh at other people's bad luck, since the people who end up suffering are elitist bullies and twits.

But things get more complicated as the Bad Thing gets closer to us—when the protective barrier of comedy begins to disappear. Look at legendary stand-up George Carlin. Lots of his jokes were centered on one stomach-churningly hilarious idea: that humanity's tendency toward self-destruction is entertaining. As he explained in an interview with Dennis Miller: "I have no stake in the outcome

anymore. I don't care what happens to you. I don't care what happens to your country, I don't care what happens to your species."

The result of the recent US election has thrown this sentiment into cruel relief. When danger, or the threat of danger, is suddenly made more immediate—does that change anything about comedy? *Should* it?

It's easy to concede that, given the amount of global suffering, the whole enterprise of comedy is somehow unfair. We've all heard someone say, "Who could laugh at a time like this?" And if you think long enough about what routinely goes on in the world, it can become hard to think of *any* laughter as something other than a cruel distraction.

But comedy is an art, and there are plenty of touchy-feely, probably super-unfunny sentiments frequently expressed about art: that it heals, that it opens the mind, that it brings us together, that it's anti-fascist. Laughter can ease people's pain and raise their spirits; it happens every day.

Whether that laughter stems from experiencing a Bad Thing—be it distant or immediate, personal, second-hand or global—probably depends on the listener. If we all laughed at the same thing, it would be boring. But comedy is a sprawling community, and there's room for everyone.

Slipping on a banana peel has been a joke for over a century, having first appeared on film in Charlie Chaplin's *By the Sea* in 1915.

Photograph: Aaron Tilley, Set Design: Sandy Suffield

MEMORABLE MOMENTS

For over 240 years, Royal Copenhagen's passion for blue has been carefully hand-painted onto delicate porcelain.
Each finished piece is a stage for your own memorable moments to play out, and over time becomes something to treasure forever.

ROYAL COPENHAGEN
PURVEYOR TO HER MAJESTY THE QUEEN OF DENMARK

www.royalcopenhagen.com

For one photographer, an unusual concern: how to create images that are not too beautiful.

Julia Hetta describes herself as a romantic. She appreciates beauty and says she falls for it easily. It seems a fortunate disposition for a photographer, but Hetta, being Swedish, also observes *lagom*—the concept of "just the right amount."

In Hetta's photographs, subjects that are obviously beautiful—flowers, fashion models—are subsequently tempered by items a touch more grotesque. For example, she managed to slip two pints of milk and a tin of sardines into an advertising campaign for Anya Hindmarch and a sheep's skull into a commission for Le Bon Marché.

Even in her personal work, fish heads, half-eaten bananas and dead birds appear regularly. "When you work with beauty, it's important that there's also an ingredient of darkness," she explains. "It's important not to make something too sweet."

Hetta has exhibited in European galleries and been commissioned for fashion editorials by magazines including *AnOther*, *T Magazine* and *Acne Paper*. She trained in Amsterdam at the Gerrit Rietveld Academie and the influence of the Dutch Golden Age weaves through her portfolio—particularly in her fascination with still lifes. Painterly, thanks to her use of natural light and long exposure times, these compositions are often, she says, a more direct nod to the Old Masters.

She often uses flowers from her own garden. She and her husband split their time between an apartment in central Stockholm and a summerhouse—"a little house"— in the Swedish hinterlands. The surrounding nature has had a growing impact on her well-being and, in turn, on her work.

"I remember the first summer that we had the country house. From being someone who didn't really care so much about having green fingers, I came to be very interested in everything that grew there—plants, seeds and so on," she says. "It was a revelation when I started to put my fingers in the ground."

Hetta now not only creates still lifes for work. Dotted around her home are tableaux that are there for no other reason than for her pleasure. She arranges flowers from her garden—appreciating their abstract forms and fragility—and creates various scenes around the house that change from week to week. "For me, just putting things in different places is a way for the home itself to stay alive," she says.

JOHN CLIFFORD BURNS

Julia Hetta

Photograph: House + House Architects

PIP USHER

Memory of Color

Why is it that humans can perceive a million colors but only remember a fraction of them?

"What if, when we talk about the color red, we all see a different color and no one knows?" is grade-A amateur philosophizing that is usually followed by head-scratching. But it is a question that has commanded the serious attention of scientists: How do humans see and understand color?

Scientists estimate that the average human can perceive a million different colors. We have the ability to do so because our eyes have three types of specialized cells—called cones—that are predominantly clustered in a tiny patch on the retina. When wavelengths of light hit the retina, these cones decipher the varying lengths and help translate them into identifiable colors in the visual cortex of the brain. Along the way, our brains factor in numerous variables that could affect this interpretation of what the eye is seeing.

In 2015, the internet went into meltdown when a photo was posted on Tumblr that showed a seemingly innocuous dress. Was it a white dress with gold trim, or dark blue with black? As millions of people vehemently divided into team white or team blue—with Taylor Swift chiming in on Twitter that the entire debacle was making her feel "confused and scared"—it highlighted the fundamental importance of context when it comes to understanding color.

"If you look at the same red shirt in bright sunlight, in a normally lit office and in a very dimly lit restaurant, the wavelengths of color that reach your eye will differ tremendously," says Madeleine Gorges, a graduate student in the University of Houston's psychology department. According to Gorges, our brains utilize visual context—such as a dark room that throws shadows on a shirt—to maintain a perception of color constancy. "In order for us to correctly interpret the world around us we must be able to identify it as the same shirt in each different context," she adds.

The dress was, in fact, blue and black; a bluish tint to the lighting had wreaked havoc with people's perception. But along the way it revealed two interesting things: Not only can our own perception be skewed without the necessary contextual aids, but it's possible to look at a color and experience something entirely different from a friend.

Our grasp on color becomes more tenuous still when we try to recall it by memory. Human memory is functional, not photographic, so we understand color by looking to other colors as a reference point. When that is taken away, and we are left only with the murkiness of our own memory, we flounder. "An exact wavelength of color is difficult for humans to recall because it does not contain any meaningful information," Gorges says.

Instead, we're able to recall only tens of colors from our full color palette of one million. Although it sounds like a hindrance, Gorges cites the numerous advantages of storing color concepts rather than a vast array of specific hues. "Think of how much processing power it would take to recall all the millions of colors," she says. In other words, our brain operates more efficiently this way—and there's no real gain to be had from remembering more.

"Having a family was an equally creative thing to do," says artist *Kiyomi Iwata*. She shares her advice on how to create art while on the seesaw of children and career.

RACHEL GALLAHER

Kiyomi Iwata

Reflecting on raising children and pursuing a career as a textile artist, Iwata repeats a favorite quote: "Life really doesn't start until the kids go to college and the dog dies."

Kiyomi Iwata draws strength from undermining expectations. A creative force raised in an era in which Japanese women were encouraged to stick to social norms, Iwata followed her own path. She has created a portfolio of pieces that not only play with the boundaries between art and craft, but also reflect her meticulous attention to detail and a life balanced between two cultures.

Like many in Japan, Iwata's family prized scholarship over creativity. "In Japan, it's acceptable to pursue art if you come from a family with a history of artists," she explains. "I did not." What she did possess was endless curiosity and a fierce urge to create.

After moving to the United States in 1961 under the guise of wanting to study English ("There were Hollywood movies and I was kind of dazzled"), Iwata met and married her husband and the pair moved to Richmond, Virginia. It was there, while taking a recreational batik dyeing class at the Studio School at the Virginia Museum of Fine Arts, that her passion for art was reignited.

"After all those years of not making anything, I really felt a connection between my heart, hands and mind," she says. Even after becoming a mother, Iwata found ways to maintain a balance between her work and life, but for many years she lost the luxury of being selfish with her time. "Having a family was a big challenge," she explains. "When my two daughters were little, it was the height of the women's movement and many friends and colleagues opted not to have children. Having a family was an equally creative thing to do, but the gratification came in a longer range."

Iwata chiefly uses three materials: silk organza, metal and *kibiso*—a rough fiber made from the waste left over when silk is pulled from a cocoon. Highlighting the enigmatic delight of mystery, many of her pieces contain vessels (with either boxlike forms or the inclusion of *furoshiki*—traditional Japanese wrapping cloth), some include Japanese *tanka* poems, others are empty. The *kibiso* pieces, woven forms often dyed or embellished with paint, seem to harness an active energy. But at the same time, the wide gaps of their weave leave space for contemplation—something Iwata has time for now that her children are grown. "I *never* thought I would just give up my art," she notes. "Art making is so emotionally connected with who I am that giving up was just never an option."

Photograph: Robert Severi

ICONIC ALESSI

by Molly Mandell

Alberto Alessi has produced a number of coffeemakers that function much like those developed by Alfonso Bialetti, his grandfather. "I decided to create the first Alessi Moka coffeemaker, the 9090, as a tribute to him and an attempt to improve on his creation," Alessi says. "It has been in production since 1979, has been a Compasso d'Oro winner and is part of the permanent design collection at the MoMA." This coffeemaker (top), designed by Richard Sapper, was followed by La Conica (middle), a collaboration with Aldo Rossi recognizable for its whimsical cone-shaped lid. Most recently, Alessi released Pulcina, a design by Michele De Lucchi (bottom). Alessi's stovetop espresso makers, much like Bialetti's original Moka Express, are a handsome marriage of contemporary design and functionality.

Moka Express

In a world filled to the brim with complex coffee-making machinery, the classic Moka Express remains a much-loved staple.

The Moka Express is ubiquitous in Italy, anchored to the stovetop of nine out of 10 Italian kitchens. The rest of the world is no stranger to this humble espresso maker either—over 270 million Moka pots have been sold internationally, and it features in the permanent collections of both New York's Museum of Modern Art and London's Design Museum.

Its inventor, Alfonso Bialetti, was born in 1888 in the sleepy lakeside town of Omegna, Italy. As rumor has it, he began developing the Moka Express in 1931 following a failed attempt at building a motorcycle. Bialetti was not a designer but a metallurgist, an entrepreneur and, according to Harvard professor and cultural historian Jeffrey Schnapp, "a tinkerer."

Perhaps for this reason, the design—despite its unmistakable octagonal form—is not exactly original. "There was a coffee service by Puiforcat and several others by Hénin that were reproduced in *Casabella*, an Italian architecture and design magazine," says Schnapp. "The designs look similar to that of the Moka Express. My suspicion is that Bialetti borrowed from these."

Even so, the functionality of Bialetti's coffeemaker makes up for whatever it lacks in appearance. Inspired by local laundry techniques and experiments derived from the first generation of larger, industrial coffee machines, the Moka pot functions thanks to a pressure chamber that pushes water through coffee grinds into a smaller container.

"The Moka Express doesn't break. It doesn't blow up or crack, which was a deficiency of many imitators," Schnapp explains. "Bialetti perfected the Moka Express a long time ago and made it so bulletproof that it developed a very devoted following."

Bialetti's invention had enormous impact, moving coffee consumption away from bars and cafés and into the home. The Moka pot's iconicity, however, cannot be ascribed to its architect alone. Its sustained success can be attributed in part to his son, Renato. Renato viewed his father's sales methods, confined to local fairs and markets, as amateur. He turned to radio and television commercials, the most famous of which included *omino con i baffi*, or "the little man with a mustache." This cartoon figure would become the company's logo and make the Moka Express internationally recognizable. The Moka Express remains almost unchanged after over 80 years despite fierce competition from the AeroPress, the Hario V60, even the Nespresso. Bialetti's coffeepot will endure as a benchmark of home brewing for coffee aficionados across the globe.

Photographs: Aaron Tilley, Set Design: Sandy Suffield

Etymology: A combination of two Japanese characters: sho ("initial") and shin ("mind").

Meaning: For Zen Buddhists, the word shoshin (which in secular parlance means "innocence" or "inexperience") refers to a beginner's mind—a state of openness and wonder that allows a person to approach life unfettered by the preconceptions, biases or habits associated with knowledge and experience. Maintaining this condition through practices such as meditation is an essential step toward enlightenment.

The paradox of enlightenment is that a person cannot attain it if they seek to do so. Unlike Western philosophers like Descartes and Rawls, who cleared their minds of assumptions in an explicit effort to gain deeper insight, Zen practitioners strive toward shoshin for its own sake, not as a tool to achieve something greater; they reject personal ambition and the trappings of intellectualism. That's not to say that shoshin equates to an embrace of ignorance: Rather, a beginner's mind is ready for and open to new ideas.

Use: The word is used throughout Buddhist philosophy, but is particularly common in the Zen tradition, notably in the writing of Dōgen Zenji, founder of Japan's Sōtō school of Zen in the 13th century. Its global usage today is attributed to another Sōtō monk, Shunryū Suzuki, who popularized Zen in California in the 1960s. The simplicity and clarity of his teachings struck a chord with many Americans and are neatly illustrated by the opening line of his seminal anthology *Zen Mind, Beginner's Mind*: "In the beginner's mind there are many possibilities, but in the expert's there are few."

Zen's popularity continues unabated, with echoes of shoshin in the ubiquitous mindfulness movement and the "disruptive" thinking of the tech industry. Steve Jobs was a Zen devotee; some argue that the intuitive nature of Apple devices and its early slogan, "Think Different," revealed his interest in shoshin. You might suggest that this commercial application of Buddhist philosophy appears to embrace the letter, rather than the spirit, of Zen—but that would reveal a failure to abandon your preconceptions.

DEBIKA RAY

Word: Shoshin

A powerful state of mind—or a paradox on the path to enlightenment?

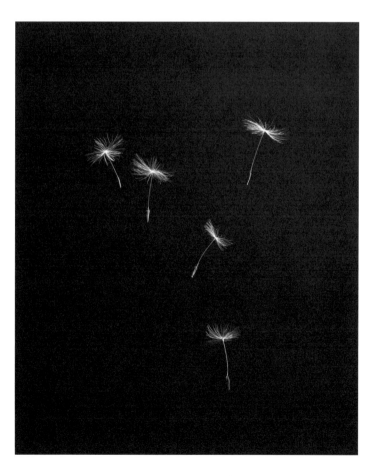

ASHER ROSS

Moses Sumney

On solitude, and the sound of leveraging lament.

"I often go up into the mountains, to write and disconnect from the world," says Moses Sumney, his cadence soft and measured, as he rides the train from Montreal to Toronto.

Solitude is a precious commodity for Sumney, and its delicate fruits are everywhere to be found on *Lamentations*—an all-too-brief but unified group of songs culled from his latest album. The EP's title is carefully chosen, like most of the words Sumney uses, and its contents find him reckoning with loneliness, the limits of intimacy and entrapment within the self.

Sumney gained widespread attention for his 2014 EP *Mid-City Island,* recorded entirely on his own with a four-track. Listeners were mesmerized by his ethereal voice and lyrics, and a swell of expectation followed him as he toured with Beck, Karen O, Sufjan Stevens and James Blake.

When asked if he feared losing control over his sound on the new album, given the arrival of collaborators like Thundercat and Trayer Tryon of Hundred Waters, Sumney remained undaunted. "The main challenge was keeping the music intimate... I wrote the melodies, all the lyrics, all the harmonies, and then found people to fill in those spaces."

Self-reliance comes naturally to him. At the age of 10, his family moved from San Bernardino, California, to Ghana, where he alleviated his loneliness by composing hundreds of a cappella songs. He still writes songs this way, choosing to enter the studio with fully formed musical concepts that in some cases exist only in his mind.

Yet he remains open to improvements in arrangement, instrumentation and other sonic nuances.

Sumney has made good use of the resources that come with wider recognition. "I wanted to show progression, and make it clear that there has been a growth, both in my tastes and interests but also in my ability to produce," he says. That determination is obvious on "Worth It," a song that stands out for its combination of a thick, honeyed vocoder effect and sparse beat. "When I put that out, a lot of people were really upset with me," Sumney says, referring to a feeling among some listeners that he was squandering his voice behind digital effects. "But a huge part of my work is vocal manipulation, and I see using a processor as part of that in order to tell a story." He's quick to note a litany of artists who have used similar devices to subtle effect: Stevie Wonder, Herbie Hancock, Zapp & Roger and, yes, T-Pain.

The song, for all of its sonic delights, is essentially a dirge—a cry from the soul. "You offer all of you / I recognize your hand as a budding bruise / You reject solitude / But I don't know if I am worth it." Sumney seized on the robotic, emotionless tone of the vocoder to enrich the song's lyrical ambiguity. "I used it as a veil to confess these really intimate things. I liked the idea of enveloping a confession in a filter, in order to make it more bearable to say or to hear."

Confession is just one mode of lamentation on the EP. Sumney also examines doubts about whether we can recover the richer selves we experienced in our youth, or realize the wild dreams we spun for ourselves. "I probably fear, often, that I'm not fulfilling the things that I dreamed I would... goals I created. They become a promised land that I don't quite get to."

Unreachable dreams aside, Sumney has come a long way from the a cappella solitude of Ghana. His shows often feature him alone on stage with a guitar, but regularly leave audiences spellbound. His voice soars and dives from a pristine falsetto reminiscent of Ella Fitzgerald, Nina Simone and Nick Drake. In particular, his style is marked by a willingness to eschew bluesy rolls, allowing single notes to modulate and die out in slow, exquisite tremolo. It's a patient style that one doesn't hear very often.

Classification can irk him, particularly when informed by racist cliché. "I'm called an R&B artist very often. We have such a strong desire to classify everything immediately in order to understand it, and I really do think we cheat ourselves when we do that. Do I really belong in the same category as Chris Brown and Trey Songz?"

In a pinch, though, he does have a preferred term: folk. He notes that while headed to the train station, a taxi driver asked about his music. "The driver goes, 'Oh, you don't look like you perform folk music.' People try to reduce you to your race when all you're trying to do is create."

Perhaps nowhere on the album is the R&B cliché dispelled more perfectly than on its final track, "Incantation," which makes use of two Hebrew texts. Sumney, who is

Sumney taught himself how to sing by listening to R&B and jazz musicians.

not Jewish, successfully evokes the ancient resonance of the prayers, yet chooses to wrap them in a darkly orchestrated tapestry of synths and strange human cries.

The song emerged from serendipity. Sumney knew that he wanted to feature a harp on the EP, and heard a woman playing one while walking home from the studio in Montreal one day. He was captivated by the coincidence, contacted the musician, and a collaboration quickly blossomed. She began teaching him Hebrew songs and he began devising ways to adapt them to his own purposes. "'Lamentations' is a very ancient-feeling word. It's a book in the Hebrew Bible. There are so many kinds of lamentations, and it felt appropriate to have this ending lament—this cry to the heavens, like, 'What's up?'"

His affinity for Hebrew has fooled several fans into assuming that he's Jewish. "I'm getting all these messages from black Jewish people, which is really cool." But he did not choose the texts in order to disclose religious feelings: "I just did it because I thought it was aesthetically beautiful. You do the thing that aesthetically speaks to you, and the meaning materializes afterward."

He claims no monopoly on interpretation when it comes to his lyrics. "I'm very adamant about saying that the lyrics mean, actually *mean*, whatever people think they mean," he says, later adding, with a touch of irony, "No matter how sad of a song I write, [some listeners] always find hope in it."

The idea of hope—and music's function in providing it—is a complex one for Sumney. Long before the likes of Solange and others became evangelists for his work, he had a fateful run-in with another star, India Arie. "She looked me dead in the eye and asked, 'Do you sing? Do you write music?' It was really strange. She gave me her email and would give me advice on my writing and what I was doing with music." Growing up, Sumney had been inspired by Arie and had planned to use his music to evoke the same hopeful, soulful messages. It was not to be: As he matured, Sumney wanted to "make the saddest possible music. I was very adamant about not writing in hope, not writing in a reso-lution to stay positive. In the end, she inspired me to do the opposite of what she did."

Sumney's pen and voice are both marked by this courage, this willingness to gaze at the limitations of love and intimacy and not blink. It is perhaps to protect this capacity that he retreats into the woods of Quebec, or Big Bear Lake in California.

"When it gets hard is when it gets good. You can't distract yourself from your own mind, and the deep, vast places that a mind can go. It's when you learn the most about yourself and about the world. It's when you're best positioned to create work and to create the work that's most interesting."

Sumney has the ability not just to unplug, but to forgo easy consolation and see life in its bruised, momentary reality. He gives few answers, and those he does provide are rich with familiar pain, familiar ambiguity. In a handwritten note above a simple self-portrait published on his website, he writes:

"Is there implied hope encapsulated in the mere expression of hopelessness? That isn't for me to determine. I'm just here to lament."

"When it gets hard is when it gets good… It's when you learn about yourself and the world."

In 2016, Sumney toured with James Blake and was a featured vocalist on Solange's *A Seat at the Table*.

2

Features

Humble, hard-working and taking on Hollywood: Rising actor *Elisa Lasowski* talks to *Pip Usher*.

Elj.isa

Photography by Stefan Heinrichs & Styling by Rose Forde

On the previous spread, Elisa wears a top by Rejina Pyo, dress by Jil Sander and earrings by Sophie Bille Brahe. Here, she wears a dress by Loewe, earrings by Sophie Bille Brahe and shoes by Mansur Gavriel.

Elisa Lasowski is not your average up-and-coming actor. Last summer, the star of salacious new period drama *Versailles*—which is, rather fittingly, the most expensive TV show that France has ever produced—found herself in Los Angeles. Instead of hanging around Hollywood, she rented a car and drove into the desert, alone, for six days. "I found a radio channel that was playing all the road trip classics like Jimi Hendrix and AC/DC and Nirvana," she recalls. There were no paparazzi-friendly nightclubs, no deluge of Instagram selfies. It was just Elisa, her car and some rock songs on the radio.

Chasing fame seems to rank low on Elisa's list of priorities. She has a private Instagram account, her Twitter presence is sporadic and she's partial to a board game in her spare time. This is a woman who may tick all the boxes for tabloid fodder—she's French, she's beautiful and she dated Charlotte Rampling's son, magician David Jarre, for years—but is carving out a career that follows her own rules.

"I don't want that kind of exposure and I think there are ways to control it," she says as she contemplates the pressures of modern-day celebrity. "There are a lot of very successful actors who are well-known, but whose private lives are intact. I don't think you'd recognize someone like Daniel Day-Lewis if he walked down the street because he's not in the media. He gets an Oscar, and then he goes home."

For someone so beautiful—and she really is beautiful: sorrowful gaze, full lips, sharp cheekbones slicing her face—Elisa is remarkably modest. There has been no quick route to fame and fortune for her, no starry-eyed chance encounter with an agent to be mythologized forever in Hollywood folklore. Instead, she has spent years as a working actor, graduating from Drama Studio London before grinding through the gauntlet of auditions, rejections and side jobs. Her first appearance as a prostitute in David Cronenberg's 2007 film *Eastern Promises* led to small roles in *Game of Thrones*, gritty British teenage drama *Skins* and police thriller *Hyena*. Now, in her current role as Queen Marie-Thérèse in *Versailles*, the uphill slog finally seems to be paying off.

"I've chosen to take an unusual path. It's definitely challenging being in a profession that's not straightforward, where you've got to hang in there for a long time before things start to flow," she reflects. "But it's amazing to do what I want to do."

Elisa's upbringing in a household that prioritized critical thinking helped shape her stance against the more superficial aspects of

Above: Elisa wears a top and trousers by Studio Nicholson and shoes by Mansur Gavriel. Right: She wears a dress and top by Joseph.

> *"It's definitely challenging being in a profession that's not straightforward, where you've got to hang in there for a long time before things start to flow."*

her trade. Born in the Netherlands to French parents, Elisa lived for several years in Algeria before returning to Holland for her formative years. As a result, she speaks English, French, Spanish and Dutch, with some Italian and German thrown in. "My parents were looking for different experiences and to go elsewhere at a time when it was not really done," she says of her "anti-establishment" high-school-teacher mother and French-literature-lecturer father. "They didn't have to seek out the international experience, but they went looking for something else."

This pursuit of the unorthodox left its imprint on Elisa and her older brother, an artist in the Netherlands. Add to that a ballet-dancing, Polish paternal grandfather ("All the men on my father's side of the family were very huge, flamboyant figures") and a Basque politician grandfather on her mother's side. Laughing, she admits that "every family has its madness and we're definitely one of the madder."

But that mesh of creative influences and cultural backgrounds is what drew Elisa toward acting. With her mother's encouragement, she acted in childhood theater productions. Harrison Ford's swashbuckling adventures as In-diana Jones cemented that aspiration, providing daydreaming material for a young imagination that thought it would be "kind of cool" to do something similar. Uma Thurman's turn as a vengeful, jumpsuit-clad assassin in the *Kill Bill* films was another dream role for a while. "It was the appeal of not only the big American movie but the kick-ass woman," Elisa remembers.

These days, her approach to her trade is rooted more in the realm of the intellectual. Each part is viewed as an opportunity to delve into a new subject matter. Sometimes, that can be rooted in practical skills, like the time she had to learn how to change a tire for a short film. "I was like, 'Yes! Now I know how to change a tire!'" she recalls gleefully.

Other times, it's weightier. Several years ago, Elisa played an Albanian sex worker caught up in a human trafficking ring. As she researched the plight of real women trapped in such circumstances, it sparked an interest that stays with her today. "Having been an actress for a few years now, what interests me about it is getting to discover a lot of new subjects that I wouldn't necessarily have delved into if I wasn't confronted by them," she says, adding, "[Human trafficking] is such a heartbreaking thing that happens in the world… I was sensitized to the subject through acting."

Elisa is quick to point out that she doesn't intentionally seek out the heavy-hitting scripts. "I work best if I can connect to a subject, connect to a director and connect to the values that the story is transmitting," she says. "But the values can be light and comedic, or dark and socially engaged."

Despite her easy smile and gentle self-deprecation, she's yet to land a part in a comedy. This could be, in part, due to her looks. While Elisa rails against the industry's desire to box its actors into neat little categories, she acknowledges that her own appearance can evoke certain sentiments. After all, there are those dark features, the pale and serious gaze. "I'd say I'd be more often typecast as melancholy because I have bags under my eyes," she says after a long pause. "I'm aware that there's a bit of soulfulness or sadness in my eyes."

This melancholia has been aptly channeled into her *Versailles* role as Spanish Queen Marie-Thérèse, a pious figure amid the rampant misconduct of King Louis XIV's court. The queen was an enigmatic and lonely figure in a court filled with gossips, social climbers and ne'er-do-wells. Commentators at the time tended to dismiss her, more intrigued by the king's numerous mistresses than a queen who liked to sip hot chocolate in her room and pray. But Elisa's research uncovered a more sympathetic portrayal from later historians— and she's applied this nuanced stance to her own interpretation of the queen as a complementary shadow to the 'Sun King's' blinding power. "[Marie-Thérèse] had a really deep understanding of royalty and what her position was," she says. "The king had a lot of respect for her as the queen—not necessarily as a woman, but as the queen."

Since *Versailles* aired on Canal+ in France in November 2015, the show has provoked an outpouring of media over its brazen portrayal of the sexual practices in Louis XIV's court. *The Telegraph* referred to the show as a "carnival of bacchanalia" and *The Daily Mail* declared that it was "the most lavishly rancid television ever screened." For Elisa, the fuss is all part of the fun: "People like to be outraged," she noted in an interview with *The Gentlemen's Journal.* "It's a very contemporary show," she explains. "It's violent, it's sexy. It has all the elements that flourish in television. And it's

No stranger to performing arts, Elisa studied both dance and acrobatics in her youth. Here, she wears a top and trousers by Barbara Casasola and a coat by Lemaire.

Above: Elisa wears a suit by Céline. Right: She wears a dress by Yohji Yamamoto, coat by Filippa K and shoes by Mansur Gavriel.

Left: Elisa wears a dress, top and shoes by Joseph. Above: She wears a dress by Yohji Yamamoto.

a period drama, which always gets a huge following. In a sense, it has the right formula to be a successful enterprise."

In fact, the show feels so contemporary that, when Elisa first read the script, she anticipated a very different kind of drama. "I thought we were going to be doing this version of Louis XIV in jeans and T-shirts, like Baz Luhrmann's *Romeo + Juliet*," she recalls. "The way we had stage directions was like, 'All of the girls are looking into mirrors as if they were taking a selfie with an iPhone.'"

Alas, there wasn't a pair of skinny jeans in sight. Instead, the cast wakes at 4:30 a.m. to begin an arduous two-hour stint in hair and makeup, after which they film all day in lavish, not to mention heavy, costumes. "There's a literal weight to what we're wearing," Elisa points out. "Women, back in the day, used to only wear corsets for a few hours each day. We get to wear them for 14 hours."

It's not just bodices and bouffant hairpieces that Elisa has to contend with on set. In the first episode of *Versailles*, Marie-Thérèse lies writhing on a bed in the midst of labor, as a roomful of courtiers look on with idle curiosity (a custom amongst French royalty that was abandoned after Marie Antoinette was nearly killed by the rush of spectators that swarmed her chamber). To prepare for the scene, Elisa asked her best friend to reenact the birth of her daughter in her living room. Next, she went online and watched birthing videos on YouTube. By the time filming rolled around, she was so well equipped that she ended up pulling a muscle in her neck as she acted out the contractions.

In the same year that *Versailles* aired, Elisa was featured in David Bowie's final music video for "Blackstar." Clad in a shabby frock with a mouse-like tail trailing out from her dress, Elisa wanders through a jagged lunar landscape until she reaches a supine astronaut, a jeweled skull inside his helmet. When Bowie died of cancer, the surreal video and its meditations on mortality suddenly took on moving significance.

Elisa's attitude toward beauty is decidedly European. She eschews the cartoonish glamor of Hollywood in favor of "looking real and looking yourself." While she admits to occasional pangs of envy over someone else's appearance, she deals with those moments with a brisk reality check.

"You must remember that you have something to offer that no one else has and that's the end of it," she says, tucking a dark strand of hair behind her ear. "That person might have bigger boobs or a better this or a more beautiful that…" she laughs ruefully. "But that's just how it is."

Like those moody shadows under Elisa's eyes. It's those shadows, and the sense of gravitas they convey, that have attracted the attention of casting agents. "I have quite big bags under my eyes that can sometimes be too heavy in photographs," she says. "But I get really upset when things are too retouched. I find it so ugly in general."

Even as she takes on more prestigious acting roles, Elisa's feet remain firmly planted on the ground. Dryly, she notes that she's seen others "eating strawberries and smoking cigarettes in the middle of rehearsal" but that's not really her thing: She'd rather keep a low profile and concentrate on her lines. There is no outlandish thespian act, no noise or drama. No look-at-me, look-at-me. "When I came out of school, I was working in a bar in Amsterdam that was underneath the theater school," she says. "I remember the students coming down for lunch and they'd stand up on the tables and start singing. I was always like, 'Is that really what I want to do with my life? Get me away from these people!'"

Unconventional and unconcerned by it, Elisa brings this quiet confidence to her roles. As *Versailles* progresses, Queen Marie-Thérèse becomes more self-assured in her isolation at court. "That's the space that she has," muses Elisa. She could almost be talking about herself: "She's her own person, in her own world, with her own objectives, and it doesn't matter who's around."

"There are so many complexities in the human psychology," says Elisa. "There are so many options, so many things we can be." Here, she wears earrings by Sophie Bille Brahe.

How to Sleep:

A Short Guide

No one really knows why we spend one-third of our lives asleep. Until recently, research into the science behind sleep has been, well, sleepy, despite booms in both sleep anxiety and the industry surrounding it. Here, *Harriet Fitch Little* goes deep into sleep to find that, much like the human body itself, there's no perfect formula.

"A good eight hours" is our gold standard. You should fall asleep quickly and wake up promptly when your alarm sounds. If you can't sleep, experiment with the thousands of tips circulating online: an herbal balm, a bath, drinking cherry juice, rubbing your tummy as you try to drift off. If nothing works, medicate. Sleep is too precious to leave to chance.

Would it be wrong to call it something of an obsession? In the same way that we now value our beer craft-brewed and our vegetables locally sourced, sleep—the most effortless of all human needs—has become a bespoke commodity, heavy with rules and anxieties. Harried city slickers pay to snooze in nap pods on their lunch breaks, phones can sync with beds to help us analyze every restless night. Globally, the sleep aid market is projected to reach $80 billion by 2020. As *The New York Times* put it recently, "Sleep is the new bottled water"—free, but packaged as a luxury.

Our sleeping habits have also become a source of unprecedented concern. Sleep for less than seven hours a day, the tabloids periodically remind us, and the risk of most known diseases increases. Sleep for more than nine hours and studies show that we are again in the risk zone—long sleepers are twice as likely to have a stroke, and rates of depression, obesity and even mortality increase significantly (the cause and effect mechanisms behind these findings remain obscure). We are so sleep deprived, and so concerned with maintaining perfect form, that four percent of American adults take sleeping pills regularly, and 50 to 70 million are currently believed to be suffering from a sleep disorder. Those numbers vary between countries, but the trend is universal. Last year, researchers at the University of Michigan declared a global "sleep crisis": Having tracked sleeping habits around the world via mobile apps, they found that there were only a handful of countries getting the recommended eight hours a night. But where did this recommended eight hours come from?

While our need to spend roughly one-third of our lives asleep is a constant, albeit a mysterious one in evolutionary terms, the presumption that we should take that sleep in one unbroken chunk is relatively new. Both historically and cross-culturally, there are huge varieties in the time, place and patterns in which people sleep. In Cambodia, sleeping happens wherever it is most convenient—a bench, a shop floor, a hammock attached to the chassis of a parked truck. Many cultures sleep in groups, drifting in and out of slumber as others come and go. In Japan, it is not unusual for employees to sleep sitting bolt upright at their desks in the middle of the working day. This form of sleep, called *inemuri*, is socially sanctioned, even encouraged—the ultimate sign of commitment at work.

In short, sleep is far more malleable than we generally presume. "Sleep is always social, affecting others and affected by others," writes Matthew Wolf-Meyer, an American anthropologist whose book *The Slumbering Masses* provides one of the most comprehensive cultural studies of sleep to date. "Society cannot exist without sleep, or sleep without social expectation."

For long stretches of time in Western societies, sleep is believed to have been a fairly broken, unthinking activity for all but the elite (who worried then as much as now about getting enough shut-eye). According to Wolf-Meyer, most people in pre-industrial societies slept in a segmented fashion, supplementing short or broken sleep at night with naps during the day. Those who studied sleep prior to industrialization generally chose to study dreams. Insomnia (a diagnosis which did not appear in the *Oxford English Dictionary* until 1758) was a concern only because not sleeping signaled possession by the devil, or perhaps a lovesick heart. It was not a public health issue: Those who couldn't sleep at night would simply catch up during the day.

Urbanization and the shift to factory labor in the mid-18th century began to slowly erode these casual patterns. Rather than setting their schedules by the sun, and by what needed doing on any particular day, urban workers woke to the summons of the factory foreman. They worked physically demanding, unrelenting shifts in environments that assaulted the senses, and collapsed into bed at the end of the day.

"Industrialization regularized sleep patterns, particularly in the early phases when everyone was woken by the factory bell and had to turn up at a particular time," says Benjamin Reiss, a professor at Emory University, whose book *Wild Nights: How Taming Sleep Created Our Restless World* was published in March 2017.

To maximize output, Reiss says, factories forced workers into longer and longer shifts. Even prior to the invention of electricity in 1879, industrialists used gas lighting to push on through the night. One striking painting from 1782, Joseph Wright's *Arkwright's Cotton Mills by Night*, shows a British factory blazing brightly in the middle of a pastoral landscape, evidence of the widespread fascination with what one contemporary commentator fretted was now a "sleepless age."

In 1817, the British socialist Robert Owen coined one of the Labour movement's most catchy appeals: Workers should spend eight hours at the factory, eight hours sleeping and eight hours doing other activities. Or, as a popular song soon spun it:

"We want to feel the sunshine and we want to smell the flowers,
We are sure that God has willed it and we mean to have eight hours,
Eight hours for work, eight hours for rest,
Eight hours for what we will."

According to Reiss, it's here that our current thinking about sleep has its origins. "Eight hours became claimed as a prerogative and a model of healthy rest promoted by the labor movement against the demands of the industrialists," he explains.

When studying sleep became a science at the turn of the 19th century, it took this eight-hour ideal as its starting point. Nathaniel Kleitman, the first man to set up a sleep laboratory, established his early theories of circadian rhythms based on the presumption that napping, dozing, waking during the night—in short everything that didn't conform to the needs of exhausted shift workers—constituted "bad" sleep. Wolf-Meyers attributes our current obsession with medicating sleep to these shifts: "That Americans now seek treatments for nightly insomnia is indebted to the structure of the American workday, and the reification of particular models of sleep embraced by early 20th-century sleep scientists," he writes.

But our fixation with sleep and "sleep hygiene"—the catch-all term for everything that contributes to the quality of our sleep—can't be solely attributed to a change that began several centuries ago.

Another factor influencing the current mood is that sleep has, over the last decade, been increasingly promoted as a revolutionary productive force. There is a growing tranche of industry leaders—Jeff Bezos and Warren Buffett among them—who boast about the amount that they sleep. Arianna Huffington exemplifies this best. After collapsing from exhaustion a decade ago and being hospitalized by the fall, the businesswoman has become sleep's number-one ambassador. Through her book *The Sleep Revolution* and through almost daily articles by contributors to *The Huffington Post*, she pushes the case that sleeplessness affects every aspect of our waking lives: our creativity, ingenuity, confidence, leadership and decision-making ability. She also makes economic arguments for sleeping more, highlighting research that says that too little sleep costs the US economy $2,280 per worker per year.

All of this bucks a historic trend: For industry leaders, sleeping less has generally been seen as the key to doing more. When Thomas Edison invented the electric lightbulb in 1879, he exalted in the fact that there would no lon-

ger be an "off switch" to productivity. "The person who sleeps eight or 10 hours a night is never fully asleep and never fully awake—they only have different degrees of doze through the 24 hours," he wrote scornfully, boasting that he personally slept for a maximum of five hours. This glorifying of short sleep stretches back in time to monks and pilgrims who would pray throughout the night as a badge of piety, and forward to modern political rhetoric: When Margaret Thatcher became the first female prime minister of the United Kingdom in 1979, her advocates never tired of emphasizing how little sleep she needed, as if barely sleeping was the ultimate sign that she truly was the equal of a man.

If there is a thread that binds these two very different moral codes, it is that both Edison and Huffington see sleep primarily as a means of improving productivity while awake.

Reiss says that the growing number of organizations that promote workplace naps for their employees are using the same framework: "Often it comes with an increase in demands on people's time rather than a decrease, so if you allow people to take a nap for 20 minutes twice a day that's posed as compensation for being in the office for 12 to 14 hours, or being on call all the time to do work on your devices as it crops up."

Reiss's personal perspective on the way we currently sleep is blunt: "It's an ordeal."

To understand what this means on an individual level, I contacted Eve Fairbanks—an American journalist based in South Africa who has written extensively about her fraught relationship with sleep. "I was never bothered by my insomnia," she tells me. "I have these memories of getting up naturally very early—waking up at five or six and just lying in bed for hours and letting my mind drift on the clouds of thoughts." According to Fairbanks, it was an increased awareness of how others slept ("I have friends who wear these wristbands that tell them whether they're in REM sleep or not") combined with a shift in her work patterns and

a doctor branding her an insomniac that made her think about her broken sleep in a way she never had before. She consulted sleep gurus, was prescribed sleeping pills and started to worry obsessively.

It's a transition that she wishes she could reverse. "When I was younger, sleep wasn't so much a part of our conversation about how we can maximize our experience of life as it is now," she says wistfully. "It feels like we don't know how to rest in modern life, to just be with ourselves. It ruins the point when one tries too hard to guide the purpose of sleep, and says, 'Okay, I'm getting sleep so I can do X better.'"

What is lost by thinking of sleep in purely productive terms?

Imagination, perhaps. Anthropologist Barbara Tedlock, who has studied sleeping patterns around the world, makes the point that there are few, if any, other societies that insist on the sharp division between waking and sleeping states that has been established in the West. For most cultures, dreams are channels of communication, moments of confession and of prophecy—places where we slip into the spiritual realm. But since the European Enlightenment, the West has seen sleep solely as a means of bodily repair, its more mysterious side too nebulous to be factored into our experiences by anyone other than Freudian psychoanalysts.

Kat Duff, who writes about Tedlock's work in her essay anthology *The Secret Life of Sleep*, describes this strict separation of sleeping and waking states in emotive terms. "Like a geological rift in the continent of Western civilization, the divide between day and night, objective and subjective, conscious and unconscious [has grown] wider over time."

When I called Duff in New Mexico to discuss her essays, compiled over the course of several years blogging about sleep, she emphasized that our insistence on the sleep/wake divide robs us of more than just dreams. Exhaustion, sleep aids and alarm clocks now "whip us into line," she says, circumventing the transition-

"Many great minds have found that the moments when we are slipping in and out of consciousness are where unusual, paradigm-shifting thoughts often appear."

al moments between waking and sleeping that have been shown to have particular creative potential. According to Duff, many great minds have found that the moments when we are slipping in and out of consciousness are where unusual, paradigm-shifting thoughts often appear. The 19th-century Swiss-born naturalist Louis Agassiz, for example, drew his groundbreaking depiction of the anatomical structure of a fossilized fish by leaving pen and paper by his bed and drawing the vision that came to him. Ironically, five-hours-a-night Edison was one of the greatest champions of this particular creative mode. While working, Edison would rest in a chair holding a metal ball in his hand. When he fell asleep, the ball would drop to the ground and wake him up suddenly. Edison claimed that in these moments he could solve problems he was unable to unpick while awake.

Perhaps the strangest suggestion of what we might be missing out on by sleeping the way we do comes from the historian Roger Ekirch. In 2001, Ekirch published his radical hypothesis that prior to electric lighting—"before sleep became a necessary evil best confined to a single interval"—people consistently woke after three hours asleep, spent an hour or so awake at around midnight, then went back to sleep.

Ekirch developed his theory after unearthing more than 500 mentions of "first sleep" and "second sleep" in texts ranging from Homer's *Odyssey* to anthropological accounts of sleep in tribal regions of contemporary Africa. He believes that the period of midnight wakefulness was most likely a time for pleasurable activities that were pushed to the margins during the daytime: visiting neighbors, having sex, reading by candlelight or simply lying awake and thinking.

Some sleep scientists support his hypothesis. In the early 1990s, a study by Thomas Wehr found that when deprived of artificial light sources for several nights in a row, subjects quickly fell into the pattern identified by Ekirch: They slept for four hours, woke for one hour, then slept for another four.

But he has his detractors. British sleep expert Neil Stanley told me that he had reviewed Ekirch's evidence, and found it wanting. "Ekirch is a historian and this is a perfect case of reification—that if something has a name then it must exist," says Stanley. He has an alternative explanation for the historical mentions of first and second sleeps that Ekirch based his theory on: "The first sleep referred to is basically the deep sleep at the start of the night. Then after that, you wake up in the second REM period, which is about three and a half hours into the night. So there's a perfectly sensible scientific explanation for what these people were writing about."

Reiss is more measured in his response. "To say that there was one default model [for sleep] is probably a bridge too far, but I do think what his work pointed out quite brilliantly is that the consolidated eight-hour model is itself a construction," he says. "Ekirch introduced the idea of sleep having a historical trajectory, of it being variable, and that really threw open the floodgates."

What can be done with the knowledge that patterns of sleep are socially as well as biologically constructed?

For some, it's a terrifying prospect. Writing in 24/7: *Late Capitalism and the Ends of Sleep*, the left-wing cultural theorist Jonathan Crary makes the case that we will soon master the need to sleep entirely. Sleep, he argues, is the last challenge for capitalism to overcome: "Within the global neoliberal paradigm, sleeping is for losers." Crary points out that the US army is now investing considerable resources into developing the "seven-day soldier"—combatants who will be able to stay awake for days on end thanks to some combination of (as-yet-undiscovered) stimulants. He believes that the technology, once developed, will trickle down into civilian life. Being a "sleepless worker" will begin as a lifestyle choice for time-poor executives, but soon become a necessity for workers trying to make ends meet. For now, at least, a sleepless world remains a merciful-

ly distant prospect. Attempts to "master" sleep, such as the Uberman Schedule—a punishing regime that involves sleeping for 20 minutes every four hours, getting a total of two hours sleep a day—generally result in participants crashing out from exhaustion.

Duff, Fairbanks and Reiss all offer similar conclusions when I asked them what practical tips might be gleaned from their research.

Firstly, in societies where nine-to-five office hours make consolidated nighttime sleeping the most obvious option, sleep disorders such as insomnia should be approached as social problems, rather than individual burdens. As Fairbanks puts it: "I think it's probably true that we have a sleep crisis, but I see it more as a crisis of society and the labor market and the way we use electricity and so on than as a health problem that can be fixed with health solutions like pills."

It's a hard mindset to shake. Fairbanks admits that despite knowing everything she knows, she still worries incessantly about sleep: "I have a shrink with whom I've been talking for weeks about stopping taking sleeping medication, and I'm so anxious about the prospect of having to go to sleep on my own that I can't even bear to try it for one night."

For Duff, an awareness of the various ways in which people sleep in different places and at different times has simply made her respect, even enjoy, the process more. "There's a lot more room for lying awake in the night than we allow for," she says. Some doctors are now experimenting with a similar strategy as a first resort before prescribing sleep aids, reassuring anxious patients that segmented sleep is not unnatural: If you're not tired when you're awake, it doesn't matter how strangely you sleep.

Sifting through the mountains of often-contradictory sleep tips with which we are bombarded, this kernel—that our nighttime ups and downs, strange dreams and wide-awake midnight moments might be "normal"—is one that bears repeating.

Day in the Life:
Adia Trischler

Adia Trischler projects a life of glamor through her work as a television host, creative director, stylist and film producer. *Julie Cirelli* hears about life on set and the difference between having it all and doing it all.
Photography by Lasse Fløde

Adia Trischler left New York City in 2007 to join her partner for a three-month stint in his native Vienna. Ten years, two children, a Vienna Stylist of the Year Award, and more than a dozen acclaimed experimental films later, she has grown into one of the city's most recognizable creative leaders and an advocate for diversity within fashion, film and television. Adia's life in Vienna is a lesson in cultivating community: She's made it her mission to unite the Viennese fashion scene around the idea of personal style, championing radical self-expression in the face of an increasingly homogeneous fashion elite. She mentors aspiring designers, both formally as a lecturer at the local fashion institute Modeschule Hetzendorf, and informally as a consultant, muse and creative director for independent Austrian designers. She's also art directed and co-produced genre-bending music and fashion films, earning accolades for her poetic use of sound and movement. Most recently, she's joined the cast of *Vienna Now* as the television show's host, where she's been responsible for introducing the cultural scene in Vienna to an international audience.

The TV show you host immerses you and your team in a variety of typical Austrian cultural experiences. What's it like representing Vienna? Viennese culture is quite staid and old-fashioned, and part of the reason they hired me was to help shift the perception of the city away from a holiday destination for old people. So here I come: I'm American, I'm black and I'm very loud. I think it has worked, but they didn't know at first whether it would. The team dynamic and energy has been good, and I get to do all sorts of fun things like go to "gay Oktoberfest" or get into a coffin or bungee jump off a building. As long as I avoid reading the horrible, trolling comments online, I love the work.

You're growing into something of a public persona. How do you navigate between the public and private parts of your identity? To be honest, I'm not altogether comfortable with being a public figure. A lot of what I do on this show is based on my personality, so I want to come across as genuine—that's why I usually work without a script. But the more I'm in the public eye, the less I can "put myself out there," so to speak. In terms of social media, this means I can't post pictures of my children. I have to protect my family and my relationship from scrutiny.

Left: Adia stands on the steps of Neue Burg. In 2014, she was featured as an insider in *Wallpaper* City Guide Vienna*.

Right: Adia starts her mornings at Palmenhaus, one of her favorite spots for breakfast meetings.

When I go out or to an event, I've got to be prepared to give it 100 percent of my energy, and if I can't do that it's better not to go out at all. As a result, I'm not very out on the scene, because if I am then I've got to be the public version of myself all the time, and that takes a lot of energy.

What's the biggest difference between being employed full time and working for yourself? When you freelance, every job is also a job interview. You have to be on all of the time because the client doesn't know—or want to know—what other jobs you have or what's going on in your personal life.

Working full time as part of a team has its own set of challenges, but it provides a certain degree of emotional stability. I feel confident that I'm trusted, I know what I'm doing, the team respects my work and I'll be paid on time. Most importantly, I'm not constantly arguing on my own behalf, and I don't have to convince anyone of my value or sell myself constantly. Working on television and in film demands a huge amount of energy, but provides a solid foundation and a strong sense of camaraderie.

When you worked as an independent stylist, did you not feel that stability? Freelance work, particularly in fashion, is its own ecosystem. It's easy to lose touch with reality when you're constantly immersed in it. When I first moved abroad and was working so hard, and getting bigger and bigger clients and projects, there was a point when I felt I was finally gaining a lot of traction. Around that time, I was having dinner with my Viennese mother-in-law and the subject of how much I was earning came up. A big commission had just come in that was very high profile but unpaid. For me, it was a great job and something of a lucky break. But she was horrified at how much work I was putting in with no financial return. To her, if you aren't making a wage off something, it's a hobby, not a career.

How much does your "Americanness" play a role in your expectations from work? The idea of the American dream is so deeply ingrained in the American psyche. That you can be successful if you just try hard enough, for long enough; and the flip side, that if you fail it's your own fault. It's the opposite mentality here in Vienna: People strive for a nice life—not fame, or riches or prestige. There's no social safety net in the US like there is here in Austria and in Europe more generally, and that has an enormous impact on the level of fear people live with. I live with that deeply programmed fear of failure, but the people around me don't seem to. It's one of a multitude of things that makes me feel foreign and other in Austria. It's a double-edged sword: On one hand, there's a lot of opportunity in the US. If you do make it, you can make it big, and you'll have all this money behind you. On the other hand, there's no other version of success, and there's not enough room for everyone to reach that goal.

And success tends to perpetuate itself, necessarily excluding others... To see examples of that you don't have to look further than many of the so-called "style icons" who have a full-time stylist working for them, pulling free clothes from all the major houses. And they can just send it back after they have worn it once. That's not accessible to the regular person. You have to be so fully embedded in that economy in order to have that opportunity. And that's not what style actually is. Style is making do with what you have, and being really good at putting things together. This reminds me of what the Studio 54 door policy used to be: mixing celebrities with completely unknown people who just seemed really interesting, and they were all in this space together. That ideal doesn't exist in many industries anymore.

Has social media changed the fashion landscape, in terms of who is inside or outside that world? People are accessible in a new way today, which makes it seem as though everyone is equal in every way, no matter how old they are and how much experience they've had. But it makes young people in creative fields feel bad about themselves, even though most of those in established careers have been working hard for 15 to 25 years or more. It's a setup for disappointment to graduate from college and then step out into the world thinking you deserve immediate recognition, and that if you don't get it there's something wrong. It's a false promise that's been made possible by social media.

Film and television by nature rely on tight, well-functioning teams. How do you keep group dynamics healthy? Almost every project I work on these days has collaborative elements, so I've had to learn how to be completely okay in acknowledging that I don't know everything and I

"I've had to learn how to be completely okay in acknowledging that I don't know everything and I can't do everything by myself."

Adia mixes vintage clothing with pieces from emerging local designers. Here, she wears a dress from 1910 and a ring from Viennese jewelry brand Heirs.

"Collaborations between groups of people aren't that different from a marriage: You want a basic foundation of dealing with stress similarly and being optimistic and flexible."

can't do everything by myself. When my role is creative director or producer, I try to set a general tone with people from the beginning, letting them know that I appreciate criticism and I tolerate it. If you don't agree with me, you can tell me, and vice versa.

Do you say it explicitly? Definitely. In the pre-production phase, there's more time to preempt future problems. But once I'm actually on set or shooting, then I'm going to be very direct when I talk to people. So I think it's important to let my team know before things get stressful what not to take personally. People who work on set or in other kinds of groups are used to this dynamic. But there are plenty of people who mostly work alone, and they tend to be more sensitive to short-mannered speaking.

What are some of the red flags to look out for when entering a collaboration? I take my cues from the first round of communication about the project: Is the attitude positive and upbeat? Do people seem to feel optimistic about the work? There are usually little cues as to whether or not the collaboration is going to be successful, and it's a mistake to shrug those off. Collaborations between groups of people aren't that different from a marriage: You want a basic foundation of dealing with stress similarly, being relatively optimistic and flexible, and knowing how to problem-solve quickly and without drama. If I can already tell from the first meeting that someone is excessively negative, or our values are not aligned, I don't take the project further.

How do you balance a rigorous work schedule with finding time to rest and regroup? There's a large part of me that is a perfectionist: I want to be a great mother, I want to be a great wife, I want my house to always be perfect, I want to be the best at my job—I want to do all of those things. This is, of course, a perfect recipe for burning out. It's why I force myself

to turn down projects if I don't feel I have enough time or energy to devote myself fully. In general, my life has so much multitasking already built into it that if I tried to balance multiple big, creative projects at once it wouldn't work.

Does having two children force you to keep things simple? After I pick up my children from school, I give all of my time and attention to them. They help me decompress, have fun and not take things too seriously.

What's a typical evening like for you? An evening at home, for example. Almost every afternoon starts in the huge park near our house, the Vienna Prater. The kids run around and play, climb trees and meet friends. I usually start dinner as soon as we get home. We're finally in a phase where everyone is willing to eat the same food, so I'm not cooking for a pre-teen and a baby and two adults. My older son has reached an age where he can appreciate subtleties, so I enjoy exposing him to good music and film. I might put a kid-appropriate experimental film or music video on while I get dinner going, and I tell them about what they're watching while I'm cooking.

When the children finally go to bed we're like *YES! Free time!* But all we ever want to do once they're in bed is talk about them and look at pictures of them on our phones. We're so lame! Especially when we tell them we need some time by ourselves, and then all we do is keep prattling on about them once they're asleep.

"I need some time by myself to think about you." Exactly! Right now, I spend quite a few evenings working, but also reading a lot. I have a strange fixation with the history of the European monarchy, so I've got a stack of books about the 12th century and I know a lot of trivia. No one ever wants to discuss it with me, though, and my husband thinks I'm weird.

We don't watch TV. We did the whole Netflix thing, but I stopped watching Netflix when I realized how time-consuming it was. The list of things to watch just kept getting longer and longer. It started to feel like a never-ending to-do list instead of entertainment or inspiration. After a long day, there's a tendency to put on something pointless and just tune out while it plays, but that's not how I want to live my life.

Do you find it easy to let go of work when you're at home with your family? I can be very hard on myself and my days are long. I wake up at 5:45 every morning and by time the kids go to sleep, I'm tired. I know there are emails to reply to, but I can't. I'm done—really, really, really done. Yet I find myself having to fight the urge to feel guilty when I'm resting because there's always something to do. I could be washing clothes, I could prepare the stuff for school tomorrow, I could write or respond to mail. But to actually sit back and think that it's okay if that doesn't get done—I'm not great at that. My husband is better at it, and as a result, he is a more peaceful person. I tell myself that you cannot do everything perfectly all the time. I am saying this. I am repeating it. But I don't totally believe it yet.

Some have an easier time with this than others... I feel like I see this with women a lot, particularly with some of the women in my family. They cannot chill. Just a generation ago, the men in my family were still not expected to lift a finger around the house. The women worked and did the housework and took care of the kids. That's not how it works in my household: My husband cooks, cleans and is an incredible father.

There's subtle messaging to women—to everyone, really—that if you're not using all of your time to the fullest, that other people are better than you are or have it more together than you do. It's also like, wait a minute, I'm working hard all day and doing a good job. Why is it not okay for me to just sit still sometimes, and not feel ashamed of that?

Left: Adia has provided creative direction and production in music videos for Kendrick Lamar, King Khan and Like (of Pac Div).

Dance

In 1968, at the height of the civil rights movement, *Arthur Mitchell* founded Dance Theatre of Harlem. His vision remains one of the most democratic in dance. *Words by Djassi DaCosta Johnson*

In moments of extreme injustice and frustration the most impactful art is born. This is true of the inception of one of the most influential American ballet companies of the last five decades, Dance Theatre of Harlem.

Arthur Mitchell created the company in New York City, after making history in 1955 as the first black principal dancer at New York City Ballet. He was also the famed protégé of George Balanchine—the Russian-born dancer, choreographer and co-founder of the School of American Ballet. Mitchell's impulse to start Dance Theatre of Harlem is said to have been spurred by the assassination of Martin Luther King Jr. on April 4, 1968.

Working in Brazil on a commission from the American government to assist in the founding of the National Ballet of Brazil, Mitchell decided to return to the US to try to make a difference in his community by teaching ballet classes in his native Harlem. At the height of the civil rights movement, in a graceful moment of artistic resistance, he created a haven for dancers of all colors who craved training, performance experience and an opportunity to excel in the classical ballet world.

The early days were humble and inclusive. Mitchell began by teaching dance in a converted garage in Harlem, leaving the doors open so passersby could see what was going on. He relaxed the dress code to encourage enrollment by young men who preferred to dance in jean shorts and T-shirts. To accommodate his growing roster of students, he eventually partnered with his former ballet master Karel Shook to help him run the school and direct what would eventually become Dance Theatre of Harlem. The company would grow to have a lasting impact on the American ballet scene and become a beacon for black dancers worldwide. It was a pioneer in the dance world, integrating stages and spreading the art of ballet through massive outreach programs at home and abroad.

A budding ballerina named Virginia Johnson met Mitchell while a student at the NYU School of the Arts and became a founding member of Dance Theatre of Harlem and, later, its artistic director. "In that first company we were an extremely diverse group of people," Johnson says of the early days. "We were Asian, Mexican, black... I think the first white dancer didn't come until 1970. But it was not about making a 'black ballet company.'" She continues, "It was to make people aware of the fact that this beautiful art form actually belongs to and can be done by anyone. Arthur Mitchell created this space for a lot of people who had been told, 'You can't do this,' to give them a chance to do what they dreamed of doing."

The company gained momentum in the midst of the Black Power movement, Johnson recalls. "But there wasn't a sense of militancy around the idea of making black people visible in this art form. It was more that he made dancers aware of the fact that they could define their *own* identity. That they didn't have to be defined by somebody else's perception of them."

The roots of ballet are steeped in the Renaissance and Baroque eras in Europe, specifically France under the decadent rule of Louis XIV. Ballet was created for nobility, to be performed *by* nobility, and it took many years for the art form to become accessible to the wider public. Even today, it is performed by a select and well-trained few. By the 19th century, ballet had spread from France to the world stage and grew as a technique in Europe and the Americas. If for no other reason than the intense training required and the elaborate aesthetics, ballet remained exclusive for several hundred years. Perhaps because so much of the early form was devoted to portraying the European idealist outlook and history, the assumption was often made that non-white dancers could not understand or embody something presumed alien to them.

The America into which Mitchell was born in 1934 was rife with racial division. This atmosphere dominated the dance worlds too, offering little opportunity for

Images courtesy of Dance Theatre of Harlem

Right: Arthur Mitchell stands in front of the Metropolitan Opera House in New York City. Dance Theatre of Harlem performed its first season at the Metropolitan in 1985.

Arthur Mitchell created a space for a lot of people who had been told, 'You can't do this.'"

Dance Theatre of Harlem performs
Concerto Barocco, choreographed
by George Balanchine. The company
premiered this ballet, its first Balanchine
piece, in 1970.

Left: Virginia Johnson dances in Glen Tetley's *Greening*. Johnson is now artistic director at Dance Theatre of Harlem.

Right: Arthur Mitchell partners with Diana Adams for the pas de deux in Balanchine's *Agon*.

dancers of color to study and flourish in classical ballet. One of the people trying to expand the art form and promote integration was George Balanchine, who would later become a mentor to Arthur Mitchell. In 1933, the dancer Lincoln Kirstein wrote a letter to a director in Hartford, Connecticut introducing his new friend, Balanchine, and their joint aspirations to start a ballet. Kirstein called for a core of "16 dancers, half women, half men, half white and half negro." What resulted was the creation of the School of American Ballet and New York City Ballet, founded by Kirstein and Balanchine. However, their joint plan for student diversity was never realized: Administrative forces that opposed the idea of an integrated ballet company consistently blocked them.

Despite resistance, Balanchine managed to bring several black dancers in as guest artists. He created *The Figure in the Carpet* for the famed Martha Graham–trained dancer Mary Hinkson in 1960, and choreographer Louis Johnson performed with the company in the 1950s, among others.

Although Mitchell is often credited as the first black ballet dancer in NYCB, a little-known dancer named Arthur Bell was a student at the School of American Ballet in the late 1940s and performed with NYCB before making a career for himself in Europe. His story was all but forgotten by history when, in 1994, a reporter found him living in a homeless shelter, alone and destitute. Sadly, his story highlights the lack of opportunity faced by many black dancers after retirement.

Mitchell had found his path to ballet as a young boy in Harlem. His mother enrolled him in tap classes at the Police Athletic League. A guidance counselor encouraged him to audition for the High School of Performing Arts, where he was encouraged to pursue ballet. He excelled at it, earning a scholarship to the School of American Ballet soon after graduation. Mitchell met Balanchine at the school and within a few years was invited to join the company.

"Balanchine was interested in African-American dancers, but Mitchell was not just a dancer to him," Johnson recalls. "He was the realization of an idea that Balanchine had wanted to explore. When Mitchell joined NYCB, it released something in Balanchine. He started creating some of his greatest work—a different kind of work, something he'd been wanting to do for some time."

Balanchine choreographed specific roles for Mitchell when he was a principal at NYCB, including the world-renowned and groundbreaking pas de deux in *Agon*, and the role of Puck in *A Midsummer Night's Dream*. Balanchine knew what many great choreographers know: that some of the best work is inspired not just by a great technical dancer, but by a well-rounded individual that can offer their own insight into the execution of the choreography.

In 1971, Dance Theatre of Harlem, billed as a "neo-classical bal-

"He made dancers aware of the fact that they could define their own identity."

let company," officially debuted at the Guggenheim Museum to great acclaim. Later the same year, Balanchine and Mitchell co-choreographed the piece *Concerto for a Jazz Band and Orchestra*, which offered an unprecedented collaboration coupled with a platform for the emerging Harlem-based company. After a prizewinning television special that Mitchell choreographed, *Rythmetron*, the company had their first full season in New York in 1974.

Mitchell rose to fame as a principal dancer with NYCB from 1956 to 1969. When he left, he seemed to rebel against the homogenous world he had been immersed in, envisioning a larger space for dancers like himself to thrive. Virginia Johnson recalls, "Right from the beginning it was about diversity in the richness, which was very oppositional to the way that ballet was moving in the 1950s, '60s and '70s in this country. At that time, 'sameness' was what was signified in ballet. One of the things that Arthur Mitchell was doing was creating the chance for people who had the skill—and the training—to perform, to keep challeng-

ing themselves, and to grow into world-class artists, which was not something that was happening in many other places."

When Mitchell began Dance Theatre of Harlem, Balanchine gave him the rights to several ballets. This afforded Mitchell a repertoire of recognizable modern classics for his programs, which was invaluable for the fledgling company. Mitchell started Dance Theatre of Harlem with a strong base, and by 1979 it was touring internationally with a repertoire of 46 ballets. In the 1980s, the company reached the forefront of the American ballet scene by carving a niche for themselves and infusing new life into works like *Firebird*, *Giselle*, *Scheherazade*, *Bugaku* and the infamous *Agon*.

Through the 1990s, Dance Theatre of Harlem continued to break racial and political boundaries, to worldwide acclaim. They were the first American ballet company to perform in Russia after the fall of the Soviet Union, and in 1992, they made an international statement on their tour to South Africa at the tail end of apartheid. The company performed to a

Left: Arthur Mitchell and Karel Shook founded Dance Theatre of Harlem following the death of Martin Luther King Jr. in 1968.

Images courtesy of Dance Theatre of Harlem

The company performs *Creole Giselle*, a restaging of the classic ballet by Frederic Franklin. The piece, created specifically for Dance Theatre of Harlem, reimagines the story with a focus on black Americans in 19th-century Louisiana.

mixed crowd and brought their outreach principles to the townships, creating a dance program that still thrives today as Dancing Through Barriers. This remains an excellent example of the impact a predominantly black and brown ballet company could make on international politics, challenging antiquated racist constructs through the simple act of practicing and sharing their art.

After 25 years as a principal dancer with the company (and a 40-year international career), Virginia Johnson returned to fill Mitchell's shoes as the company's artistic director in 2013. "When Arthur Mitchell invited me to step into his huge shoes, I really didn't want to," she says. "But I knew that the work needed to continue. There's a particular challenge right now. In 1968 and 1980 and 1990, the novelty of Dance Theatre of Harlem and the extreme difference of the experience was something that was very powerful, whether audiences were used to going to the ballet or not. Nowadays, we're in an electronic age where we don't really understand or even appreciate the notion of the live performance of an art form that is so rigorous. One that requires actually coming into the theater."

Dance Theatre of Harlem went on hiatus due to financial difficulties from 2004 to 2012. "This means that there was a generation of little girls who didn't see brown ballerinas," Johnson says. "They didn't have that seed planted of *I could be up there too! I want to be a part of that!* So we really need to rebuild that sense of inspiring another generation of dancers to come forward."

Johnson has been instrumental in helping usher the company into a new era while maintaining the old legacy. Dance Theatre of Harlem is not just a ballet company or groundbreaking cultural institution, but an elegant example of what is possible when an inclusive approach to art is allowed to evolve and thrive.

Left photograph: Danilo Scarpati, Right photograph: Paola Pansini

At Work With:
Dimore Studio

In an industry distracted by just-so austerity and asceticism, Dimore Studio designers *Britt Moran* and *Emiliano Salci* are waving a flag for indulgence. As soul mates, business partners and muses to one another, the daily working relationship between Moran and Salci is much like their interiors: intimate, unconventional and often quite dramatic. *Words by Pip Usher*

Left: Dimore Gallery in Milan features
contemporary and classic furniture
either handpicked or designed
by Moran and Salci themselves.

Right: Casa Fayette, a hotel in
Guadalajara, marries Mexican
design with traces of Dimore Studio's
Italian heritage.

Britt Moran has a problem with clutter. Unlike most interior designers'
modish obsession with minimalism, however, the co-founder of Dimore
Studio finds every corner of the crimson-walled home that he shares
with his creative partner, Emiliano Salci, jammed full of pretty things.
"I was thinking the other day how I constantly order books. I have books
coming every other day," he sighs. "I can't possibly put another book
anywhere. It's the same with objects and small trinkets. Maybe it's part
of the interior design problem: You're constantly going to markets for
your clients and you'll see a piece of fabric and think, 'I want a meter
of that for myself.'"

These magpie tendencies have seen the dapper pair build a formi-
dable interiors business that champions their anomalous approach to
design. "The word 'dimore' in Italian means dwelling, but conjures up
images of old villas clinging to their aristocratic origins," says Moran,
adding it lends the name "a sense of nostalgia." Based in Milan, Salci
and Moran are surrounded by the grandiose relics of history; many of
their projects riff on this environment with striking results. In the 13
years since Dimore Studio was founded, they have designed interiors
for some of the world's chicest brands and count fashion houses Hermès and Bottega Veneta, restaurateur Thierry Costes and hotelier Ian
Schrager as clients.

Moran and Salci start each of their projects by creating a fictional
person to guide the narrative. Once they have settled on a character,
they create a mood board adorned with images from art, design, fashion and architecture to visualize an imaginary world. Describing his
creative process, Salci explains: "The first thing I do is look at the space
and then, almost immediately, I can sense what I wish to do. My inspiration comes from the world around me—the streets, exhibitions and
museums I visit."

At the start of 2016, the duo transformed luxury skincare label
Aesop's second Milan store into an old-world apothecary. Throughout

The Dimore duo feel grateful that they can bounce ideas off one another; many colleagues of Moran (left) and Salci (right) work independently.

the process, they imagined "the governess or butler of a well-heeled Milanese family, who visits the space to restock the bathroom linen closet or kitchen pantry with all the sundries necessary to maintain that faint perfume that hangs in the air of the house they're servicing." This fantasy manifests itself at every touchpoint in the store: arched display cabinets, tiled in green; lemon-yellow shelves; a stainless steel sink tucked in one corner. In the center sit two mid-century chairs in a dusky shade of pink velvet. "We experiment a lot with color and the relationship between the various colors we use," Moran adds.

Moran and Salci hope this scrupulous attention to detail will create a lasting impression long after customers have left the shop through its heavy glass-fronted doors. "I think retail spaces are moving away from just the standard globalized concept and people now like having very specific stores in different cities," Moran says. "It becomes a tourist attraction in itself."

The duo has a particular fondness for hospitality projects because of the all-immersive creative freedom that such commissions allow. "The hotels and restaurants are interesting because you really have to think about how someone responds to the environment that you're creating," Moran says. "It has to be functional, it has to be interesting, it has to be timeless."

Last year, Guadalajara—a city in western Mexico famed for its tequila and mariachi music—also became known for Casa Fayette, a 1940s colonial mansion that the pair transformed into a retro-inspired, defiantly colorful hotel. Throughout, they imagined Luso-Brazilian samba singer Carmen Miranda "arriving at the hotel with trunks of clothes, singing late into the night on the patio and having breakfast by the pool the next day late in the afternoon."

With Miranda as their muse, the hotel was steeped in sultry, old-world glamor. In the common area, there are salmon-pink walls and a low sofa in a deep shade of purple; at the hotel's bar, Tropicália-print chairs and gold tones amp up the air of sun-kissed decadence. The somewhat spartan hotel bedrooms are dominated by strips of color, like the mint-green headboards that frame crisp white bedsheets.

"We try to push our clients as much as possible with colors, materials and items of furniture from different eras," says Moran as he reflects on Dimore Studio's approach to design. "I think that's our DNA: We take a historical approach to a project to give it some roots, and then we inject it with more of a contemporary feel."

Although Moran hails originally from North Carolina, he has lived in Milan for so long that his English is occasionally flecked with an Italian slant. "My one year off has turned into 20," he laughs, recalling how he fell in love with Italy's fashion capital after visiting decades ago as a college student. He and the Tuscan-born Salci met through mutual friends and immediately connected. Both worked in creative industries—Salci as creative director at Cappellini, Moran as a graphic designer—and quickly began to collaborate on projects. By 2003, they had founded Dimore Studio and, two years later, had launched their own furniture line (their sumptuous pieces are shown at Salone del Mobile each year). As their clout has grown, so too has their company: Today, they preside over a team of nearly 30.

Their shared vision stretches beyond the parameters of a traditional business partnership. The two men have lived together in their shared home in Milan "forever," says Moran, making them housemates as well as a creative team. A demanding workload, coupled with the industry's numerous social engagements, means that they spend most waking moments together. But despite the intimacy, their relationship remains platonic.

"I know—it's a really strange arrangement," Moran says. "I really do think that in order to get everything done, that's how it has to be. We start talking about everything in the morning, we have lunch together, we have dinner together. We have our own line of fabrics, a furniture design company, we participate in international fairs, and then there are all of the projects. So to get everything done, you basically have to eat, sleep and breathe the studio 24 hours a day."

"Our life is centered on what we do," adds Salci. "We work 24/7 because we enjoy what we do so much. It seems natural to work at the office and to take our work home."

"The word 'dimore' in Italian means dwelling, but conjures up images of old villas clinging to their aristocratic origins," says Moran, adding it lends the name "a sense of nostalgia."

At Casa Fayette in Guadalajara, hand-selected vintage finds, like these wire pool chairs, are paired with furniture from Dimore Studio's own catalogue.

FEATURES

Over the course of two years, Moran and Salci transformed a five-story mansion in Paris' Second Arrondissement. Once home to King Louis XV's foreign minister, the space has been repurposed into the art deco–inspired Hôtel Saint-Marc.

Like any close relationship, there are dramatic blowups, particularly when the two are faced with the industry's demanding deadlines. For Moran and Salci, the trick is to clear the air: "I think a good shouting session helps sometimes," Moran advises. "We have a great group of people that we work with and it's kind of like a family. And, as in every family, there's usually a good shouting session, then we all kiss and make up and go have a drink together."

After more than a decade, the pair have settled into their respective roles as business partners. Salci—a vision of European excess in extravagant prints and wild socks—is the designated "crazy genius" while Moran—clad in more neutral clothing—"has to be there to make sure the client thinks we're going to move through the projects." As Moran has assumed responsibility for the administrative side of things, handling contracts and interactions with the press and lawyers, it's left Salci "with the liberty to be a little less burdened."

Their yin and yang personalities are underpinned by a shared sense of industriousness. "We're very, very hands on, and I think that's one thing the client really expects from us," Moran says. "We don't just delegate projects to junior staff and expect them to generate it… It's a lot of work. To have certain projects look the way you want, you have to be very diligent and meticulous."

The scope of their ambition shows no sign of slowing down, with several projects in New York currently in the pipeline. As their acclaim grows, Moran admits that the unique intimacy of their partnership provides a comforting constancy. "At the moment, I'm really happy to have someone to bounce ideas off," he says. "It would be a very daunting position to be just the one person."

> "We have a great group and it's kind of like a family. And, as in every family, there's usually a good shouting session, then we all kiss and make up and go have a drink together."

Left photograph: Simone Fiorini. Right Photograph: Philippe Servent

DIETER RAMS:

"As little design as possible."

Dieter Rams discusses the people and principles that have made him a design legend. *Words by Alex Anderson*

The German language has a useful ability to unite ideas in a single word that somehow exceeds the capabilities of its parts. *Industriekunst* is one of those words. It's translated into English as "industrial design," but this loses the crucial senses of balance and fusion implied in the German word. Industry-art would be closer. The pioneering German industrial designers of the early 20th century perceived in this conceptual union of the practical and aesthetic a liberating force for the imagination. They felt its potency in their ability to evoke delight in functional objects. This radically simple idea has stood as a challenge to every modern designer—and a promise to every consumer—for more than a century.

Dieter Rams, head of product design for Braun from 1955 to 1997, met this challenge and delivered its promise more capably and comprehensively than perhaps any other designer of the late 20th century. His designs for radios, calculators, clocks, kitchen appliances and furniture make them quietly understandable and agreeable. These seemingly modest attributes derive from an intense effort, Rams says, to "return to simplicity," to abandon the designer's ego and to fight the market's "ruthless exploitation of people's weakness for visual and haptic signals." So, his products explain rather than announce themselves, their buttons and dials invite rather than demand adjustment and their colors and textures gently serve these ends. Each refinement finds more effective ways to use industrial processes and optimize material, so that manufacture and aesthetics resonate together.

A deep ethical current flows through Rams' thinking and ripples into the products he designs. Its primary force is discipline, a word Rams uses to express the constraint a designer must exercise to "omit the unimportant," let products express themselves and allow users to take their own pleasure in them. These goals contribute to a larger moral imperative: to enrich human life in a way that encourages holding on to things, rather than always seeking the new or the spectacular.

This is a global struggle against excess, waste, visual pollution and environmental destruction. Since his retirement, Rams has continued to advocate these values forcefully in essays, interviews and exhibitions—and later this year in a documentary film—reasserting that design must serve rather than dominate people, and that it must help us feel comfortable with fewer things so that we can resist wasteful exploitation of material and energy. "We need new structures for our behaviors," he declares, "and that is design." For Rams, industry-art must not only evoke delight; it should also guide ethical thought. Design historian Klaus Klemp refers to Dieter Rams as one of the two great bridges of modern design. If earlier designers carried the traditions of art toward industry, Rams carries industry toward the home and civil society. Dieter Rams recognizes the responsibility of designers to activate the liberating capacities of industriekunst and to enlist useful and agreeable objects in service of people and the planet.
—

You were an early pioneer of sustainability in its broadest sense, and a critic of wastefulness, visual pollution and triviality in design. Now that environmental sustainability has been in the public consciousness for a while, these broader issues are beginning to come around again. Would you agree with Lance Hosey, an architect and author on aesthetics and sustainability, who declared, "If it's not beautiful, it's not sustainable. Aesthetic attraction… is an environmental imperative"? Beauty, not just appearance, that is both exemplary and instructive, certainly intensifies and prolongs the relationship with the user and therefore

Published by Phaidon in 2011, *Dieter Rams: As Little Design As Possible* is a comprehensive monograph of Rams' work and includes specially-commissioned photographs of his home in Kronberg.

TEN PRINCIPLES
by Molly Mandell

Dieter Rams began expanding, ever so slightly, his "Less, but better" mantra into concise principles about what constitutes good design during the 1970s. He started with three principles at a lecture in 1975, and by 1985, the list had grown to its current 10. Though straightforward, these commandments are iconic and continue to serve as inspiration for many designers, including Muji's Kenya Hara and Apple's Jonathan Ive. Rams' ideas about design continue to be well-documented today by publishers like Phaidon, who in 2011 produced a near 400-page book on Rams' career titled *Dieter Rams: As Little Design as Possible.*

1.
Good design is innovative.

2.
Good design makes a product useful.

3.
Good design is aesthetic.

4.
Good design helps us to understand a product.

5.
Good design is unobtrusive.

6.
Good design is honest.

7.
Good design is durable.

8.
Good design is consequent down to the last detail.

9.
Good design is concerned with the environment.

10.
Good design is as little design as possible.

Previous page: Photograph © bpk / Abisag Tüllmann

"They should ideally stay in the background, like a valet in the old days that one hardly noticed," Rams has said of the products he designed for Braun.

AT HOME WITH DIETER RAMS

by Molly Mandell

Filmmaker Gary Hustwit's documentary RAMS, which will be released in fall 2017, will be the first feature-length documentary about the life and work of Dieter Rams. Over the course of 18 months, Hustwit was granted rare access into Rams' life, including his home. "He's created exactly the world that he wants to live in," says Hustwit. "Visiting is like entering his head. His house is filled with his designs—everything from the furniture to the stereo system to the appliances. He even made closet doors." Rams' design influence extends beyond his own home: He is responsible for the urban planning of his neighborhood in Kronberg, Germany. In the early 1960s, Braun enlisted Rams to help plan a housing development for the company's employees. Rams' home, which borders the Taunus mountain range, has an unsurprisingly minimalistic interior. Aside from Braun and Vitsœ products, Rams collects Japanese art and ceramics. Hustwit explains, "I think his love for Japanese design stems from its connection to nature. Most people don't associate Rams' work with nature, but it's something that is very important to him. His ideas about reducing visual clutter are also connected to letting surroundings inform aesthetics."

also makes sense ecologically. In my 10 principles of good design, I have written that the aesthetic quality of a product is an integral aspect of its usefulness, for the appliances that we use daily have an impact on our personal environment and influence our sense of well-being. But a thing can only be beautiful if it is also well made. Of course, there are general criteria of beauty such as harmony, contrast or proportions, but individual aesthetic sensibilities can vary a lot and can also depend upon knowledge, education and awareness. This is why I have always tended to steer well clear from this discussion about beauty and argued instead for a design that is as reduced, clear and user-oriented as possible and simply more bearable for a longer period of time. But "simple" is especially hard to achieve; even Leonardo da Vinci knew that.

Does a conflict between practical utility and abstract beauty still encourage innovation in product design, or are there other more assertive mechanisms at play? Calm, sober and intellectual surprises should always be possible with design. Practical value and beauty are not mutually exclusive, even today, and they are unlikely to be so in the future either. For me, a restrained aesthetic and function that is as optimized as possible have always been important. These qualities lead to long utilization cycles: The objects do not become visually unbearable after a short time because they have not pushed themselves into the foreground. Certainly, these qualities also act as a constraint upon innovation. We really should consider very carefully whether we constantly need new things. I have been arguing for a long time for less, but better things.

Early on, artists, critics and manufacturers perceived two key benefits of industrial design: It made products both more desirable and more profitable, and it contributed to a general improvement of public taste. You seem to perceive a third benefit of industrial design, which is that it reduces wasteful consumption by producing objects that people will like and hold on to, which in turn benefits the environment. Do you think the consumer product industries feel a con-

"'Simple' is especially hard to achieve; even Leonardo da Vinci knew that."

flict between those earlier goals and this newer one? I completely concur with [German architectural and art critic] Adolf Behne that we need "comfort" instead of "luxury." He believed that really good design should not be fuel for consumption that brings us nothing but irreparable resource problems and environmental destruction. There has been much and persistent talk about sustainable growth; it's time to do something about it! The only plausible way forward is the less-but-better way: back to purity, back to simplicity. Simplicity is the key to excellence!

A number of authors have noted that your work was influenced by the Bauhaus. It seems more productive to think of your work as fulfilling the promise of Peter Behrens, widely considered the world's first industrial designer and mentor to Mies van der Rohe, Le Corbusier, Walter Gropius and many of their contemporaries. Very early in his career, Behrens declared that there is "a liberating quality" to the union of practical utility and abstract beauty because these were so often in opposition to each

other in his era. Part of his success later, it seems, is that he capitalized on overcoming this opposition—with appealing and often surprising results. During your career at Braun, did you sense any continuity with the pioneering efforts of Behrens in his role of creative consultant at German industrial design company AEG? During the relatively short period of his position as artistic consultant to AEG, between 1907 and 1914, Peter Behrens did indeed—as one of the first industrial designers ever—have the opportunity to shape many areas of that company. What he succeeded with, above all, was overcoming historicism and also to a certain extent Jugendstil, which was so prevalent at the time. For me, his enduring achievement was that he showed clearly the value of collaboration between top management and design. When I arrived at Braun in 1955, their products were still conceived by engineers and detail engineers and censored by salespeople. In the early years, we began working on a more modest product language that derived from function but was stripped of the formal mendacity that was

commonplace at the time. This was thanks to the appreciation and support given to design by the top management—in particular, Erwin Braun himself. In this respect, there were clear parallel design goals to those of AEG.

I was most certainly aware of the Bauhaus culture during my studies at the College of Applied Arts in Wiesbaden. The founding director, Professor Hans Soeder, had based the school's curriculum on Bauhaus principles. Particular role models were Mies and Gropius, who had also both worked as assistants in Peter Behrens' office.

Are there products that you use regularly and that you particularly enjoy, or that you think exemplify the principles of design you developed and refined over the years? My wife and I live in our house furnished predominantly, but not entirely, with products from Braun and Vitsoe. For example, the Vitsoe 606 Universal Shelving system: I designed it 56 years ago and still feel comfortable with it. When you live with products, you get to learn their faults so you can improve them and thus keep the designs alive for longer!

The 606 Universal Shelving System that Rams designed for Vitsœ is still in production some 50 years after its conception and is thought to most successfully convey Rams' design principles.

3

Weekend

Spring

Clean sheets, fluffy towels and long-lost socks: an ode to the small triumphs of laundry day.

Cleaning

Photography by Zoltan Tombor, Styling by Alpha Vomero & Set Design by Sam Jaspersohn

Makeup: Bryan Zaragoza, Hair: David Cruz

Previous spread: Tarah wears a top by Creatures of Comfort and trousers by Andrea Jiapei Li. This spread: She wears a top by ICB and trousers by Issey Miyake.

Right: Tarah wears a dress by Samuji. Overleaf: She wears a dress by Edun.

Left: Tarah wears a top by Tibi, skirt by WRKDEPT, trousers by DKNY and shoes are stylist's own.

Above: Tarah wears a dress by Acne Studios. Right: She wears a shirt and dress by Tibi. Overleaf: A top by Milly, trousers by Andrea Jiapei Li and shoes by A Détacher.

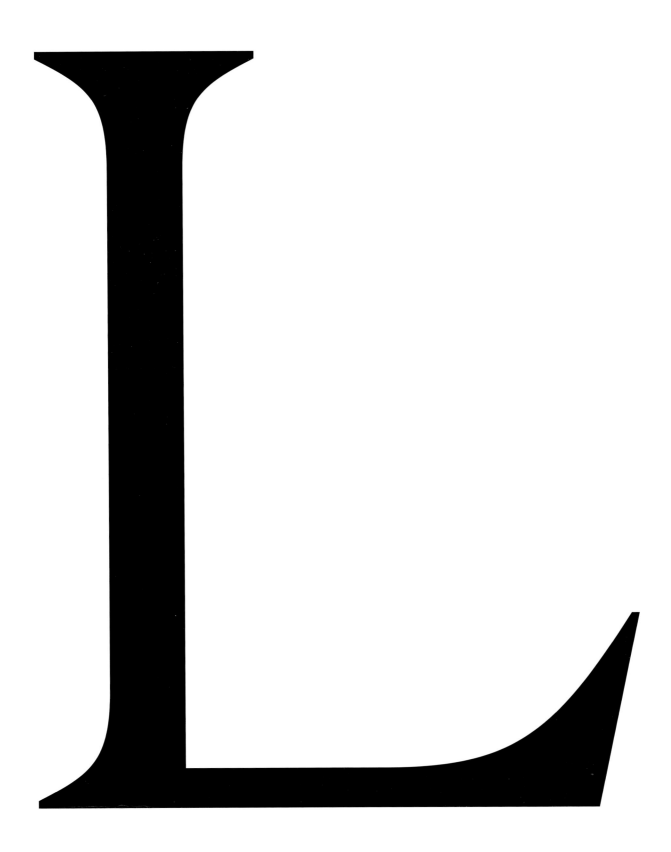

Composer Leonard Bernstein spent the summer of 1967 in Ansedonia, a sun-washed Roman town on the Italian coast. There, he would bathe on hot stones by the lapping sea before returning to his family's rented villa in the evenings. The Bernsteins regularly declined invitations to attend dinner parties in favor of rest and leisure—of reading or playing a hand of cards together in the shade of the orchard or plunging into the pool. The days passed slowly and began to revolve around the Tyrrhenian Sea. The summer had followed an exhaustive period of work, and Bernstein found the body of water restorative. "And there was the sea, which he loves. To submerge himself in water, to be weightless and at one with its forces, produces feelings of supreme contentment within him. When he emerges from the sea he seems resuscitated both physically and spiritually," wrote author John Gruen, who along with photographer Ken Heyman, accompanied the Bernsteins on that summer vacation, documenting its energy and playfulness in *The Private World of Leonard Bernstein*.

Bernstein delayed his vacation so that he could conduct an orchestra on Mount Scopus in Jerusalem. He was the last of his family to arrive in Italy.

The Bernsteins' vacation in Italy was a new experience; they had spent every other summer on Martha's Vineyard or at their country house in Connecticut.

WEEKEND

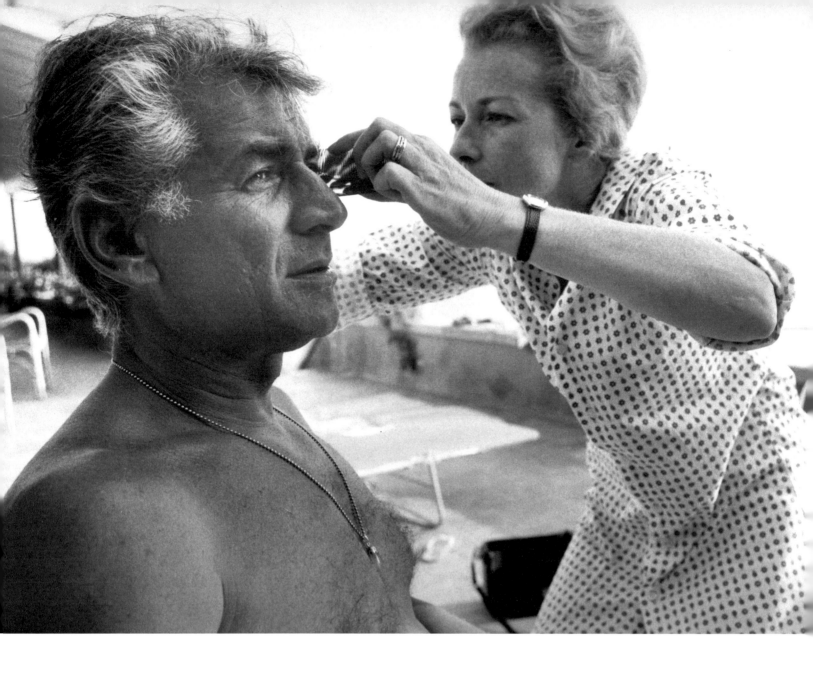

During his time in Ansedonia, Bernstein worked on a commission to compose the inaugural opera for the John F. Kennedy Center in Washington D.C.

The Sweet Sorrow

of Rereading

Rereading books is like meeting old friends: The characters we thought we knew challenge us to incorporate fresh understanding. "Seeing former classmates at a twenty-fifth high school reunion can come as a shock; so can reseeing a once beloved book," observes author *Patricia Meyer Spacks*, who in the name of research spent one year reacquainting herself with novels first encountered in previous chapters of her life. Here, in an extract from her book *On Rereading*, she expounds on the simultaneous pleasures of stability and surprise derived from rereading. *Photography by Kenneth Josephson*

If you're a parent, grandparent, aunt, uncle, cousin, or friend of the family, you've perhaps endured the fury of a toddler compelled to listen to her favorite book with a word missed or a picture skipped. The point of the favorite book, for the listener, is that it remains the same. The more often the three-year-old hears the familiar sentences, the more content she appears. When a word changes, pleasure recedes: A beloved book has lost its identity.

Trying to account for this passion for sameness, we may say that it reveals the toddler's need for security. In a world crammed with new experiences, exciting yet unpredictable, the child treasures what she can hold on to. If even the book turns unpredictable, she loses what she has depended on. A friend's personality has changed. We smile grown-up smiles at the child's demand for perfect reiteration even if we retain that childish need in more acceptable form, addicted to our own rereadings.

Diverse impulses motivate us rereaders, desire for security among them. Consider Larry McMurtry, writing in his early seventies: "If I once read for adventure, I now read for security. How nice to be able to return to what won't change." McMurtry reports that publishers keep sending him new books to comment on. He sends them back, preferring the books he already knows. "When I sit down at dinner with a given book," McMurtry writes, "I want to know what I'm going to find."

We always find frustration: Early in life, the adults we depend on won't read the book to us exactly as it should be each time; later, we realize the impossibility of rereading, re-encountering, regrasping, everything we have already perused. But we may discover, also, the special, increasingly complicated pleasure of literary re-encounters. Rereading: a treat, a form of escape, a device for getting to sleep or for distracting oneself, a way to evoke memories (not only of the text but of one's life and of past selves),

a reminder of half-forgotten truths, an inlet to new insight. It rouses or soothes, provokes or reassures. And, as McMurtry reminds us, it can provide security.

What kind of security, exactly? McMurtry suggests that a book reread offers what will not change—but for most readers, rereading provides, in contrast, an experience of repeated unexpected change. We remember Hansel and Gretel making their trail of bread crumbs, but it may come as a surprise to reread the Grimm brothers' version of the story and find the witch licking her lips over the prospect of eating the children on toast. Only a tiny detail, that, but one that complicates the story's flavor and makes it memorable in a new way. That allusion to toast makes the reader suddenly aware that the witch really is planning to eat those children.

She's thinking about the meal to come. I read the tale anew in the battered copy of *Grimm's Fairy Tales* that survives from my childhood and come upon this unexpected moment. Did I fail to remember it because once it scared me by its specificity? Who knows?

Change occurs not only as a result of noticing new details but also because interpretations alter. In a youthful reading of *Crime and Punishment*, Raskolnikov seems a daring young man, exciting in his willingness to defy convention. As a grown-up rereader, I think him a fool, or a monster. I read the novel again: He has become an object of sympathetic pity tinged with horror. I find myself enthralled for new reasons.

Sometimes a book changes for the worse. Vivian Gornick: "When I read Colette in my twenties, I said to myself, That is exactly the way it is. Now I read her and I find myself thinking, How much smaller this all seems than it once did—cold, brilliant, limited—and silently I am saying to her, Why aren't you making more sense of things?" We read to recap-

ture the thrill of a book first encountered 20 years earlier, and the thrill has mysteriously vanished. We remember a wonderful story, and the story has turned into a cliché. The change may attest to our maturity, but it feels like loss.

Or, perhaps, provocation. As Verlyn Klinkenborg puts it, writing in *The New York Times*, "The real secret of rereading is simply this: It is impossible. The characters remain the same, and the words never change, but the reader always does. Pip is always there to be revisited, but you, the reader, are a little like the convict who surprises him in the graveyard—always a stranger" ("Some Thoughts on the Pleasures of Being a Re-Reader," May 30, 2009). Klinkenborg claims that the books he repeatedly rereads provide not a canon but a refuge. In other words, this special group matters to him not because he judges its members to be of particular merit but because its books supply a certain kind of emotional satisfaction. His manifest excitement at the role of the reader—always a stranger—suggests, however, that his satisfaction involves more than refuge.

The question of what kind of security rereading offers gives way to another: How can rereading provide security at all? How can a rereader who remains "always a stranger" expect reassurance?

If books keep changing along with their readers, they possess no stability and would seem to offer no security. Seeing former classmates at a twenty-fifth high school reunion can come as a shock; so can reseeing a once beloved book. Yet the claim of security carries conviction. It reminds us that in every book, though much may change, much stays the same. The plot no longer thrills, but it remains the plot that thrilled us once. The characters appear more or less reprehensible than they did before, but like those high school classmates, they continue to possess traits we recognize.

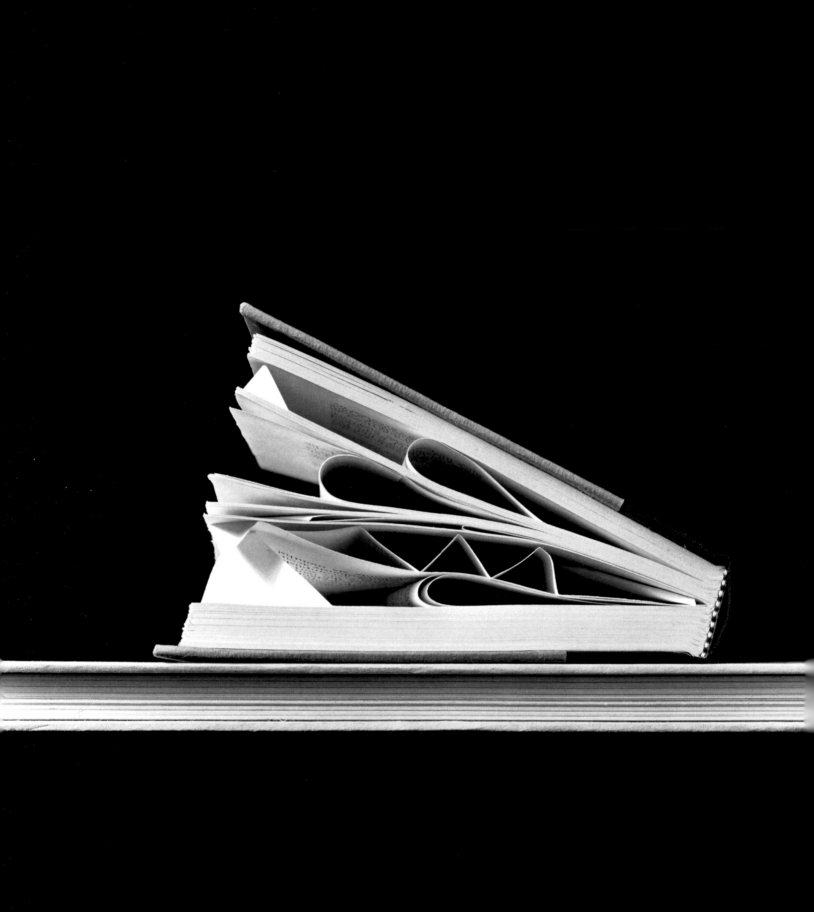

WEEKEND

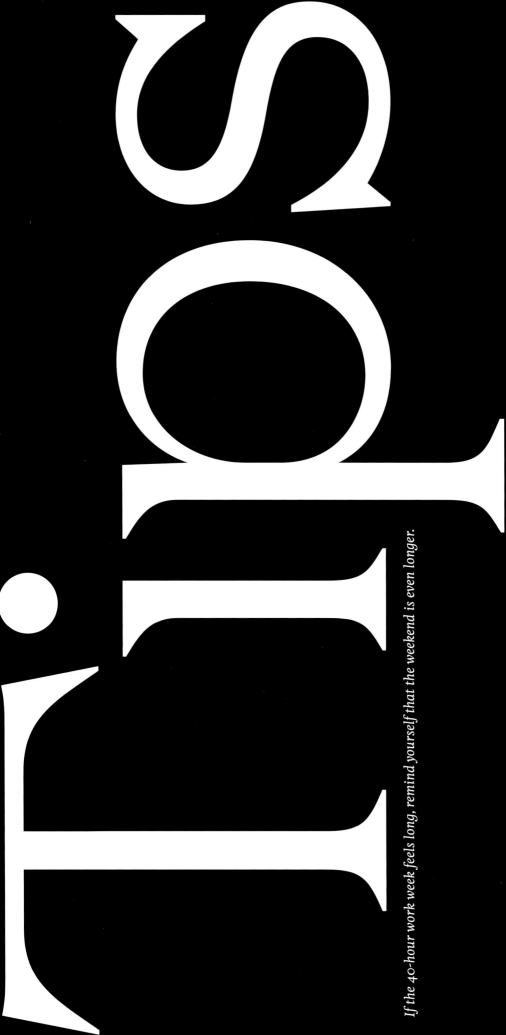

If the 40-hour work week feels long, remind yourself that the weekend is even longer.

Words by David Plaisant, Asher Ross & Tristan Rutherford & Illustrations by Frédéric Forest

Words by Asher Ross

Get Outside

James Joyce, with his usual penchant for modesty, once said that a genius is incapable of making mistakes, that "errors are volitional and are the portals of discovery."

However true this may be for art, Joyce's words have a lot to teach us when it comes to navigating the physical world. The ubiquity of Google Maps and other navigation systems has significantly reduced our experience with being lost. There are obvious advantages to this change, but scientists and laypeople alike are now taking notice of the downsides. One seems certain: that we learn less about our physical world when we are guided through it passively, and we have fewer opportunities for the lucky discoveries that come from finding our own way. We are less likely than ever to happen upon the wooded byroad that gives us a more pleasant commute, or the cheerful pub that lies nestled a few miles beyond a well-known route.

For most of their history, human beings have been remarkable navigators. In his book *The Lost Art of Finding Our Way*, Harvard physicist John Edward Huth explores the extraordinary navigational techniques of ancient cultures, including Arabs, Pacific Islanders and the Norse. The latter of these encountered Greenland, Iceland and Newfoundland through navigational errors that have now become the stuff of history.

Huth emphasizes that there is no objectively correct method for navigation and that ancient humans, having to improvise without a constant GPS signal, created all sorts of ingenious ways to stay on track. Natives of the Caroline Islands used something called the etak system in which, during long journeys at sea, they would envision imaginary islands along the horizon in order to measure their progress against the stars. The 13th-century Norse *Hauksbók* includes instructions for reaching Greenland from Norway using only descriptions of the sea and sky.

What all ancient navigators had in common was the capacity to create "cognitive maps"—mental images of their environment that were accurate enough to allow them to improvise and reorient in the event of trouble. It is precisely this capacity that is threatened by dependence on route-planning software.

It is difficult to know exactly how much this change has influenced our sense of well-being, but it has likely led to physiological changes in our brains. One study, conducted in 2000 by neuroscientist Eleanor Maguire demonstrated that London taxi drivers, people who have to create and maintain very detailed cognitive maps, had more gray matter in the hippocampus region of their brains. The hippocampus plays a complex role in memory consolidation, spatial navigation and the emotions.

One leading researcher in the field, Dr. Julia Frankenstein of Technische Universität Darmstadt in Germany, is quick to remind us that these changes are not permanent. "The cost of our dependence, like all dependencies, is freedom, and the gain is security… If you don't use navigational strategies, if you don't actively remember your environment and don't develop cognitive maps, you get worse at it."

Frankenstein, who avoids mapping services herself, emphasizes that using Google Maps proactively, and avoiding its route-planning aspect, can help us cultivate our own cognitive maps and become more self-reliant. She recommends several experiments to this end.

"Play a game: Look at a map, plan a route in your mind, and see how long you can follow that route without having to resort to your map again. Take a navigation system with you if you must, but it's better to experience uncertainty." She also notes some spur-of-the-moment tests we can impose on ourselves. "Take a detour at random. Jump out at a different metro station and try to get home. Or draw a map of your hometown and then compare it to a real map. Examine the distortions. What did you miss?"

She admits that social norms make some of these experiments difficult. In order to develop a richer cognitive map, one has to be willing to make mistakes and to be late from time to time. While Frankenstein says that cognitive changes are reversible, she worries that related social expectations may present a more difficult obstacle.

Still, the potential rewards are inviting. Developing an internalized map of our home and its surrounding regions can give us a unique sense of agency, of being grounded both emotionally and physically. It can give us a feeling of connection with our ancestors, who could easily point north without the aid of a smartphone. Cognitive maps are part of how we understand ourselves and feel at home in our bodies. The hippocampus, after all, is central to memory formation, and it is a battleground for conditions like Alzheimer's disease and schizophrenia.

On the bright side, as data accumulates on the detriments of route-planners, some researchers have rolled out projects that seek to improve them.

New services could help build cognitive maps rather than replace them by highlighting spatial information and requiring proactivity. Some could even teach map-reading skills to children. Google has points A and B locked down. The challenge now is finding those portals of discovery.

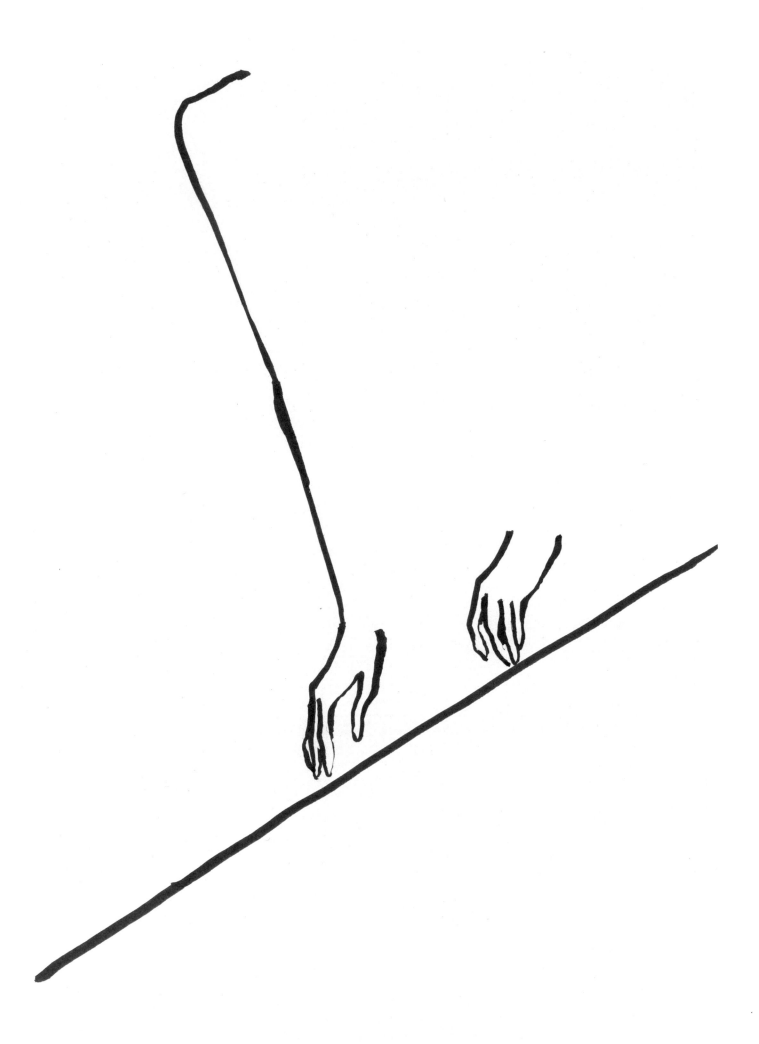

My wife and I just spent the entire weekend in the nude. Stark naked. In our birthday suits. Au naturel. As naked as the day we were born.

The only word I can use to describe the experience is "easy." It was easy to jump in the shower or to get ready in the morning. When naked together we felt uninhibited. While alone we felt childlike. It was dreamy, introspective. It felt good.

We're doing nothing new. Such mindful nudism slapped Europe on the cheeks when the first Freikörperkultur (FKK, or Free Body Culture) movement was founded in Germany in 1898. Physical and psychological balance was at the movement's core. Nude archery and tug-of-war were considered good for the body; hiking naked through nature—whether solo or in a group—good for the soul. It was also a chance to wash off the smog of the Industrial Revolution, if only for an afternoon. A day to undress the stresses in pastoral bliss. Hitler tried to ban the FKK. Hermann Göring, a Nazi Party leader, claimed, "One of the greatest dangers for German culture and morality is the so-called nudity movement." They lost that battle. So too did dictators of a later era. FKK bathing on beaches of the German Democratic Republic become a riposte to communist conformity. What could be more liberating than baring your buttocks to tyranny?

Our minimalist mentor is Greek philosopher Diogenes of Sinope. As a retort to societal straightjackets, he led the simplest life he could. That meant wearing not a stitch of clothing. His finest hour was when he ditched all of his possessions except a single wooden drinking bowl. But poor old Diogenes was shocked when he saw someone drinking from a fountain by cupping his hands. "Fool that I am, to have been carrying superfluous baggage all this time!" The Greek then smashed his wooden bowl and was thus encumbered by nothing. That's exactly how my wife and I felt last weekend. Friends who grew up in everyday naturist households seem devoid of bodily hang-ups—perhaps ever more important in today's social media–saturated world. Those incubated nudists seem content within their own skin in a wider sense. Unstressed about sex. Confident in their conduct. Kind to a body they actually know. Some might call such behavior shameless. I call it without shame.

One can offer few tips for indoor nudism. Its obviousness mirrors its sheer simplicity. Benjamin Franklin liked to take "air baths" by an open window as soft breezes awakened his senses. I'd like to think that his naked contemplations inspired his inventions like the lightning rod, bifocal lenses and swimming flippers. Fellow American polymath Walt Whitman summed up our own naturist tendency: "There come moods when these clothes of ours are not only too irksome to wear, but are themselves indecent."

Be Naked

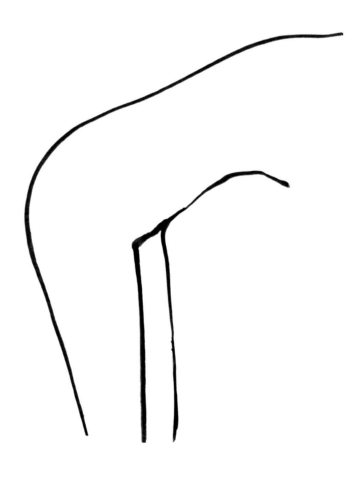

Words by Tristan Rutherford

Words by Asher Ross

Help Others

Crises and political shifts around the world have induced a sense of hopelessness in many people. Never before have the needs of the marginalized and disenfranchised been so clear, yet there remains a strong temptation to turn inward.

It's only human to desire comfort—to zone out with our headphones on or dive deep into the arms of television drama. It's worth remembering, however, that there are limits to the happiness that such activities can bring. Dr. Dan Ariely, professor of psychology and behavioral economics at Duke University and author of *Payoff: The Hidden Logic That Shapes our Motivations*, notes that "in general, none of us are very good at predicting our own happiness." He suggests that we often succumb to something called the hedonic treadmill—the pursuit of pleasure that provides only fleeting gratification. Pleasure is a great motivator: We don't need a reminder to crave a milkshake, a glass of wine or a cigarette. But our appetites aren't so good at recalling altruistic sources of happiness. Though most of us have experienced the rush of joy that comes from giving to others, it's easy to forget how wonderful it feels.

We might realize that we should get out and help others on the weekend, but we don't often get around to doing it. What can we do to change our patterns of thinking? For one, we can understand that certain types of altruism are more powerfully motivating than others. Ariely recommends "the kind of things where you get to see the impact you have on other people. Something like a soup kitchen, where you see the person who is getting food." He juxtaposes this to things like philanthropy and preventative efforts. While both are potentially virtuous, they do not give the same in-the-moment glow that can encourage ongoing commitment. So start simple. Start with something that will make you feel happy right away. Some might say that focusing on the pleasure we take from helping others undermines the virtue of the act. But by cultivating our desire for altruistic joy, and by paying close attention to the fulfillment we experience, we give ourselves a better reason to do good in the future. Ariely describes this goal as a state in which "the structure of [our] happiness is built on other people's happiness."

The incentives for working toward this structure are strong. There is the immediate good done for those in need, and then, of course, the joy we derive from acting in accordance with our principles. But there is a third factor, and one that is perhaps just as important: By giving our time to others and being happy as a result, we act in defiance of those who see the world as a zero-sum game, who think any gain comes at a cost to someone else. Empathy does not consume or take away in order to give joy. It's a miraculous aspect of the human spirit. We are lucky to have it, but it requires cultivation.

Do Nothing

Recently I ran into a friend who, although well, seemed a little vacant. I asked her what she was doing and her breezy reply charmed and intrigued me in equal measure. "Oh nothing," she told me with an air of contentment and a broad grin, "quite literally nothing at all!" On that crisp autumnal mid-morning we found ourselves in Rome, just a few blocks from where I live. Doing nothing is, in fact, a core tenet of Roman culture, but as you might expect it is not actively promoted. The culture of *far niente* (to do nothing) permeates and influences the primary functions of city life. But far niente doesn't always mean irksome idleness or an arrogant indolence. In Rome, doing nothing is an activity, and as if to justify its presence, those who take part tend to be masters.

As all Romans know, sloth is one of Catholicism's Seven Deadly Sins; this sin, however, is most open to interpretation. Theological definitions and spiritual significance surrounding sloth have always been murky, from neglecting one's duties to being indifferent to the world around you. But, in Rome, to call far niente a sin would be sinful in itself. My friend was merely partaking in a key aspect of city life; all she did was to call it by its name. And for those who want to make a habit of non-exertion, this city has the perfect infrastructure for inactivity. One theory goes that Romans, being so visually spoilt and stimulated, need nothing bar a pair of eyes and a set of legs (and not necessarily the most athletic) to keep them occupied. A walk of just a few hundred yards to the piazza and back might, say, include a couple of baroque churches, the entrance way of a renaissance palazzo, various fountains, a full-to-brimming newsstand, a bustling tobacconist shop and so on. The visual and visceral intrigues are such that doing nothing, not having an appointment, or even a plan or destination is irrelevant: Your raison d'être becomes the city, and this is true of tourists and residents alike.

As such, banal experiences become urban odysseys. Having moved to a new neighborhood recently, I attempted to quench that supposedly innate need for physical activity by going on a run. Fully outfitted and programmed, route ready and morning sun shining, I was raring for my Roman run. Architecture and topography make for a jogger's enemies, I quickly discovered. If it wasn't a narrow staircase climbing around a rococo grotto, then it was a 1960s apartment complex gleaming in all its marble and bronze glory. The distractions were manifold and subsequent sporting attempts only resulted in infinitely more visual discoveries.

In a similar way, a visit to Adalberto Libera's post office—a 1933 rationalist masterpiece on Via Marmorata—inadvertently turns a menial activity into an adventure. Waiting for your number to show on the red screen becomes a secondary experience to the architectural trance induced by the lashings of polished black granite that loftily surround you.

Just as Roman infrastructure and urban beauty elegantly throw a spanner in the works of efficiency, Roman cuisine also slows the metabolism of the resident to a near glacial rate. Saturday is about eating *polpette* (meatballs)...*e basta così!* (and that's it!), you might say with total legitimacy.

Food, post offices that are a bit too beautiful and a general abundance of just about everything have all helped grant Rome an air of willful idleness at its most artistic: weekend walks that stay very much within the neighborhood and gentle jogs that are more bench-to-bench than point-to-point. Here, the far niente maxim reaches its inactive zenith when it becomes a *dolce far niente*; the sweet, blissful nirvana of disoccupation. I now endeavor to show less bemusement and more respect when I meet someone in the midst of doing nothing, because in Rome it is a hard-won indulgence that nobody should go without.

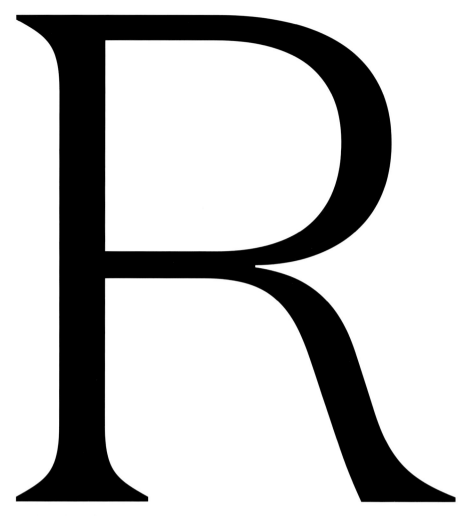

R

Rossana Orlandi has seven decades of Saturdays under her belt. In Milan, where she reigns as the doyenne of Italian design, we spend one more in her company. *Words by Sarah Moroz & Photography by Marsý Hild Þórsdóttir*

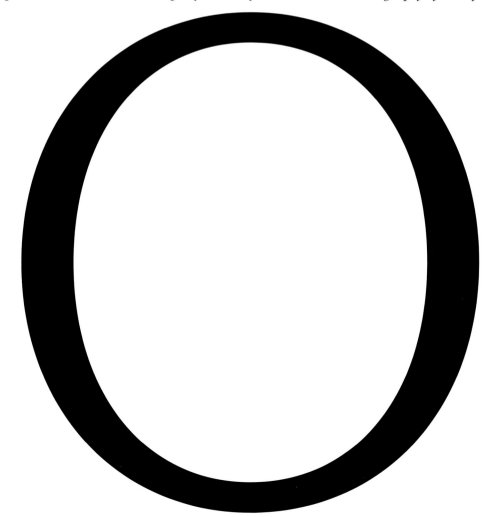

O

Orlandi's oversized sunglasses are an iconic part of her look. People often stopped her on the street to ask about her eyewear, so she started producing and selling the glasses herself.

From Via Matteo Bandello, the only hint of Spazio Rossana Orlandi's existence is a discreet yellow buzzer in a metallic frame. The neighborhood is quiet, mostly populated by established bourgeois Milanese families. You have to ring the buzzer and pass through three gates before reaching the sprawling buildings within. And, by the time you reach the first gate, it is clear that this venue is something altogether exceptional.

Rossana Orlandi, a petite Italian with pulled-back gray hair and red nails, is known for her keen eye. Not only does she spot great designers before anyone else, she also creates a gallery that is eternally theatrical, with great turnover: Pieces swoop in and out of her space in a breathless cycle. Thus, each visit to Spazio Rossana Orlandi is guaranteed to be different from the last.

"Every time something new arrives, Rossana feels the need to change everything around," chuckles her right-hand man, Marco Tabasso, who has been working with Orlandi for over a decade. Before creating the gallery, Orlandi had her own knitwear collection, keeping one foot in a longtime family trade of spun yarn production. Orlandi's sister, in fact, made a career of providing high-fashion fabrics to luxury labels. "I met Coco Chanel with her,"

Orlandi reminisces. "I was very young, Coco was very old."

Orlandi was a private collector of design items even while she was running her knitwear company. As she started to place and sell pieces over the years, the endeavor evolved into a more serious gallery enterprise. "It grew a little bit like a mushroom," Tabasso notes wryly.

The space on Via Matteo Bandello was initially tapped to be her home. At the end of the 19th century, the whole block was a brick factory called Fornace Candiani. In the 1970s, the venue was reconverted into a factory for Prochownick, the Italian tie manufacturer. The property belonged to one family, who now only owns the garden behind the building. Orlandi gets to keep its lush view.

"It has always been a place that everybody loves. All my designer friends, when they come, get ideas and want to do something. They help me develop the space," Orlandi says. The gallery retains many authentic details: storage boxes (from the "tie" era) line entire walls, and original wooden partitions are beautifully preserved in the showroom. Such vintage details counter the bright whimsy of the space with a proud sense of legacy.

There are no strict divisions between the showroom, store and gallery; each functions as a different kind of meeting point. There is a mix of things from around the world: from South Africa to Holland to India. "It becomes a kind of village of design," Tabasso says. When a new piece arrives, everything else changes around it; likewise, selling a piece means reimagining everything in its environs. Orlandi is a maestro of mise en scène, creating interesting and unexpected resonances between pieces. She develops her eclecticism by reading magazines, traveling regularly—when we spoke, she'd returned from Prague the night before—and staying connected to social media for ideas. "Online, we can be citizens of the world," she says. "Instagram is quite good, especially in a taxi."

Amidst the dizzying display is a pool table that can also be used to serve apéritifs, made by Hillsideout in collaboration with Hermelin. Nearby is a 24-hour video installation, filmed in real time at a private residence in Manhattan, which is framed on the wall like an actual window. Made by Anotherview, it offers a meditative look out onto New York City—a contemplation on the nature of urban movement and shifting light. Down the hall, the so-called Tom Dix-

on room (whose walls have been painted black ever since a showcase of the designer's work here several years ago) features pieces by Matteo Cibic for Indian manufacturer Scarlet Splendour, a carpet by Studio Job for Nodus Rug, a glass shelf designed by Germans Ermičs, and two brass mirrors by Fratelli Campana for Ghidini 1961.

The restaurant flanking the gallery is also part of Orlandi's universe—evident by the raw stone and brick mixed with assorted flourishes. To reduce the noises that echo off the vaulted ceiling, rotating design features are used to absorb the sound, like a knit rug by Christien Meindertsma for Thomas Eyck hung on the wall, or an armada of cloth dinner napkins dangling from the ceiling. The restaurant, which serves Italian cuisine, also caters Orlandi's events. Orlandi's gallery is a staple on the Salone del Mobile circuit, not only thanks to her fascinating design microcosm but equally for her reputation for ebullient entertainment. Orlandi recently finished six dinners helmed by six Michelin-starred chefs, each around the idea of spaghetti al pomodoro.

Orlandi takes a laboratory-like approach to living well. "If we speak of art, it can be absolutely uncomfortable and nonfunctional. If we speak of a chair, and it's not comfortable, then it's not a chair," Orlandi says. "It depends on what it is. Lamps can be sculptural. But if a sofa is not comfortable, it's stupid," she says.

To relax, Orlandi prefers to spend time outside of her Milanese base. "I'm familiar with more cities abroad than Milan," she laughs. She's especially fond of Naples and Copenhagen, though her most memorable travel story is from Ireland, where she spotted the strangest-looking house she had ever seen. "I wanted to see who lived there," she says. "So I rang the doorbell." While one might assume that the owner would've been thrown by an accented stranger suddenly appearing on the doorstep, Orlandi's instincts had led her to a kindred spirit. "We had a fabulous afternoon, talked over tea," she recalls fondly of the man who answered the door and remains a friend. He told her that "happiness is up to you"—a mantra she still believes in. When it comes to more localized

"Luxury is feeling comfortable. Not only comfortable, but cuddled."

Right: Orlandi enjoys showcasing young designers. Slovenian designer Nika Zupanc, whose velvet upholstered bench is featured here, has created limited edition collections in partnership with Orlandi since 2011.

leisure time on the weekends, "the best, for me, is to spend it in the country with my family," she says of her place several miles outside of Milan. The country house is a place for family gathering—she has four children, who have families of their own—and has been laid out precisely with active grandchildren in mind: "It's a super easy house, even though it's full of design," Orlandi says. "Today, luxury is feeling comfortable. Not only comfortable, but cuddled."

Alternatively, Orlandi sometimes repairs to a family castle. It has plenty of stories, although "not much in terms of design—just my bedroom," she says. Her family was "a very classical family" with a collection of beautiful furniture. "But they're antiques, which I don't like," Orlandi says. To prove the point, she let a designer transform an old family desk in heavy wood by charring it black. It's a fitting symbol for how Orlandi operates: renewing design with a sense of boldness, never treating tradition and history too reverently.

Her first important design piece was the Spoon Light by Sebastian Wrong, which she saw before it was put into production by Drove Design (later made by Flos and renamed Spun Light). "I have the original," Orlandi says. "I al-ways suggest people buy the prototypes because they are amazing." She explains, "Often, production means compromise. If you touch the light as a prototype, it's completely different. The proportions are different—thin, elegant."

Orlandi is a woman who knows what she wants. "If I don't like it, it doesn't come to the gallery," she pronounces. (To one designer, whose table she didn't feel was quite there yet, she advised, "If it was a flower, I would water it.") She doesn't adhere to any particular aesthetic criteria: If she doesn't like the color, she changes it, and she doesn't shy away from kitsch. Her team, which includes her daughter, can sometimes soften or change her point of view. "I'm quite hard and straight, but I'm not absolute," Orlandi says. "We give input, but the designers have to be free," she says, to have their own point of view. But ultimately: "If I don't like the result, that's another question."

"We've seen young designers become stars," Orlandi continues. "It's such a big pleasure to watch them grow up. We try to have exclusivity, but other people want to work with them—sometimes they're kidnapped!" Of the fact that so many big names had their first projects with her during Salone del Mobile, however, she says, "It makes us proud." Tabasso recalls the gallery's early days: "When we started, people were complaining that we didn't have so many Italians," which was mostly due to the fact that small-batch production was not the Italian norm. Local designers "had an old idea of design, which is 'I design, and the company takes care of everything and I earn royalties,'" he laughs. "But Italians now study abroad, and we mix a little bit."

If the designers are changing, so are the clients. Orlandi spots trends in buying habits through shifting social strata. "What we lost is the middle class. They don't have money like they used to," she acknowledges. Moreover, her highest-level buyers treat the act of buying differently. "They want to know much more," she notices. Spazio Rossana Orlandi is ultimately a niche market, not only between art and design but selling as-yet-unknown and internationally sourced brands. "We need to reassure the clients of a good investment." Luckily, Orlandi is a reliable barometer on that matter. "We like this idea that we're a vitrine for young designers getting into the field," Orlandi says. This is the underpinning philosophy that powers the place year after year: studying, nourishing and boosting young creativity.

Before opening her Milanese gallery and store, Orlandi spent over 20 years consulting for labels such as Giorgio Armani and Donna Karan while running her own knitwear brand.

Weekend Agenda:

Six Cities

1

Inés Miró-Sans
Hotelier, Barcelona

On weekends, I try to stay fairly close to home; the faster I can get somewhere, the more time I have there. I often go to an area in the countryside called Empordà since it's only a 90-minute drive from Barcelona. One Saturday, when I was in Empordà, I walked a trail in the mountains; there was this smell of the outdoors and I realized that I knew it from my childhood. I don't experience that sensation as often as I should. But for me, it's so valuable to connect with nature. If it's a nice day, I also love to swim in the sea. Afterward, I'll buy vegetables and meat from local farmers. There are a lot of artisans in the area, too. Recently, I discovered a man who has been making ceramics for over 40 years. We bought all the ceramics for the rooftop of our hotel, Casa Bonay, there. It's a really interesting scene and the more people I meet, the more I feel that I'm planting roots here.

I'm not a big planner. Normally, I won't know what my weekend plans are until Thursday, maybe Friday. If I'm in Barcelona on the weekend, I cook. It's the thing that relaxes me the most.

If I do leave Spain on a weekend, I stay in hotels. There will always be people who love Airbnb, and there will always be people who love hotels. I'm a hotel person. For me, Airbnb is like experiencing local housing, but without the people. I do love meeting local people, so I look for small hotels where I can get to know the owner or that share a similar philosophy to Casa Bonay. When I'm traveling, I always leave my laptop behind. Actually, I think it's important to turn off on the weekends, even if you're at home. We always have our phones open, checking things and receiving information. You can really overdose on that. Buy something at the market, go home, cook and put music on. Or just turn everything off, and you'll feel like you're on vacation without going anywhere. With technology, everything is connected, and you have this feeling that you have to do and see so much. My advice is to do one thing and enjoy it. Don't rush.
—

After spending three years with the Ace Hotel group in New York, Inés Miró-Sans returned to her native Barcelona to start her own venture, Hotel Casa Bonay. In a renovated 1869 building, Inés has created a home away from home not only for locals and travelers, but also for herself.

2

Jenna Gribbon
Artist, New York

Weekends have become an important opportunity for people to devote more time to socializing in a political way. My partner and I originally founded The Oracle Club, a membership-based salon, as a social space and workspace for artists and writers. It was meant to be a home away from home for our members—and for us—to use for working, living and gathering. With the political changes going on around us, however, The Oracle Club has taken on a new significance.

The experience of being with people who care deeply about similar things is very fortifying. New York City can be quite competitive and cutthroat, so it's vital to have a group of people that support one another. Ordinarily, during the day, people use the club as a workspace. In the evenings and on weekends, we use it to bring members and their friends together.

Lately, many of these gatherings have turned political; as artists and writers, that's what we need right now. I think we all feel the responsibility to be active and to catalyze change, to keep things moving forward. It's clear that many of us are paying the price for our past lack of political engagement, which is why we feel like our weekends are well spent when we're gathering together and grappling with the issues.

The real challenge in cultivating a community, political or otherwise, is forcing yourself to leave your comfort zone and to engage with strangers. But right now, there's no time for shyness. It's important to speak up and form alliances, to band together and make a change. Use the resources and space you have, like your kitchen. Find people with a common goal and invite them over this weekend to share ideas. You never know where that can lead.

At the very least, it would keep people engaged in conversation. It would turn us from passive observers into active participants. The important thing is to start with what you have and with who you have, regardless of how small. These things tend to grow. For us, we benefit in so many ways from having all these people who were not in our lives before. Maybe the world can, too.
—

Between 2010 and 2014, artist Jenna Gribbon painted a series of people in conversation. At the same time, she and her partner, Julian Tepper, opened The Oracle Club, a membership-based salon in Long Island City, to encourage real-life dialogue.

FREAKY FRIDAY *by Molly Mandell*

Studies suggest that certain days of the week are more hazardous than others. Most heart attacks, for example, occur on Monday, perhaps due to the stress of returning to the office. Monday, however, is not the most dangerous of days. Friday is the peak day for automobile accidents and is the United States' deadliest day, with Saturday and Sunday following close behind. Tuesday may be the week's silver lining, and not just because it isn't Monday. Tuesday is the safest and most productive day of the week and is also the best for online shopping prices and applying for jobs.

3

Enrique Olvera
Chef, Mexico City

When you're deciding what to eat on weekends, don't focus too much on health. I don't even believe in "healthy" or "unhealthy" foods, per se. Everything simply comes down to quality. Many of the things that we assume are unhealthy, like bread or cheese, are fine for the body if they are high-quality. Seeking out unprocessed, unrefined ingredients is the best way to balance comfort food and healthy living.

My family likes simple recipes, so for dinner on the weekends we often opt for a nice piece of fish, which we cook in banana leaves with a lot of herbs and some lime. We serve it with a roasted tomato salsa and eat it with tortillas. I'd say that fish tacos are our family's go-to weekend recipe.

We also love soup with chicken and vegetables on the weekends—we eat that constantly. It's an easy and complete meal if you add a little lime juice, some spice and some avocado. Keeping a garden encourages us to use fresh greens, and there's something special about pottering around in the garden on the weekend.

Another great weekend dish is mushroom tamales. They're quick and healthy. If you don't have access to masa, just roast mushrooms in the oven by themselves and add a fresh green salsa.

When I'm traveling, I do my homework. Before I leave, I read up on what's going on in the place that I'm traveling to, and I get recommendations from friends and other chefs. But there's also a real value in just walking around and discovering places for yourself. There's no need to do homework about coffee, for example. It's better to wander hungrily, and try out whatever grabs your attention.

In all things, it's good to stay loose and flexible enough to change your mind. If you wake up one morning and feel like staying in bed, you should. I like to do that, too.

—

Famous for his reinterpretations of Mexican classics—and his 1,000-day-old mole—Mexican chef Enrique Olvera's restaurant Pujol has been a mainstay on the "World's 50 Best Restaurants" list since 2011.

4

Anja Aronowsky Cronberg
Editor-in-Chief, Paris

Saturday:
11 a.m. – 2 p.m.
Eat croissants.
Read *The Guardian* online.
Bum around.

2 p.m.–3:30 p.m.
Argue with husband about bumming around. Eat leftovers or more baked goods for lunch.

3:30 p.m. – 6 p.m.
Walk around the Marais with my husband.

6 p.m. – 7 p.m.
Go to the gym and read *The New Yorker* on the bike that allows you to sit comfortably. Pedal slowly.

7 p.m. – 1 a.m.
Come home super hungry and moan about dinner not being ready. Eat when dinner is ready. (Usually my husband's pasta carbonara; if lucky it's got asparagus in it. Then proceed to ruin the flavor by adding too much chili.) Apologize about moaning. Watch illegally downloaded series or movie in bed.

1 a.m.
Sleep.

Sunday:
As above but with pancakes for breakfast.

"There's really no such thing as dressing too casually on the weekends."

KYOSUKE KUNIMOTO

Kyosuke Kunimoto
Fashion Designer, Tokyo

I often start my weekend by taking a walk. I like to walk to quiet parks and shrines, places with fewer people, where I can read a book. I love André Gide, Franz Kafka, the Japanese author Kōbō Abe. During the week I can find the time to go to my favorite places—record stores, theaters and bars—but I can't find the time to read. I think that's because I need to be at a certain place, a very quiet place, where I can enjoy the combination of literature and nature. That's my ideal spot on a weekend.

I often visit an area in Tokyo called Jinbōchō, where there are lots of vintage bookstores and record stores. Music is one of the most important forms of inspiration for my creations and my aesthetics. But at the same time, it makes me feel very relaxed; when I want to unwind from a long week, I listen to music.

I believe that suits aren't only for weekdays. I'd like to see more people get dressed up for big nights out on a weekend with a tie, pocket square, cufflinks. I'd love to see people wearing suits at cafés and bars. Wearing a suit on the weekend can make you feel different—more put together.

But I don't usually dress up on a weekend, unless I have parties to attend. I often wear a black leather sports jacket with a lapel, maybe a lighter jacket and a shirt underneath, something vintage like a western, poplin or silk patterned shirt. As for trousers, I don't wear much denim; it's too stiff and heavy for me. I like to wear a pair of broken-in cotton corduroy trousers. When I buy them, I go home and wash them until they get really soft. After 20 or 30 washes, they're very soft and comfortable to wear. That's my weekend uniform.

There's really no such thing as dressing too casually on the weekends—people should wear anything they feel comfortable in, as long as it's their style. You should always keep your style, even when you're at home.
—
Tokyo-based designer Kyosuke Kunimoto launched his label Maison Lance six years ago. He has since designed bespoke suits for clients including St. Vincent, Yoko Ono, Frank Ocean and Alejandro Jodorowsky.

Hisham Akira Bharoocha
Creative Director, Brooklyn

Saturday:
9 a.m. – 12 p.m.
Take supplements on empty stomach, as instructed. Drink coffee and eat an English muffin with peanut butter and jelly. Go to the gym with wife.

12 p.m. – 6 p.m.
Go to the farmers market to buy the week's supplies and drop off compost. Return home and prepare to face world. Leave house, one hour later than planned. Absorb art at museum or in Chelsea with friends.

6 p.m. – 9 p.m.
Discuss dinner plans with friends or my wife. Eat dinner.

9 p.m. – 1 a.m.
Either I'm in sweatpants on the bed about to watch a bunch of *Daily Show* reruns or ready to head out the door to a club. If it's the latter, I usually go to a DJ gig or a live show. Home by 1 a.m. and fall asleep on the couch, fully clothed.

4 a.m.
Switch from couch to bed.
Finish sleep cycle.

Sunday:
Like Saturday, but with less grocery shopping and an earlier bedtime.

MODERN WEEKEND *by Molly Mandell*

Unlike months, which correspond to the moon cycle, the seven-day week is an entirely human construct. Its roots are in Babylonia, but it was the Romans who popularized the idea. The weekend is a more modern marvel. A day of rest has long existed in religion, historically Fridays in Islam, Saturdays in Judaism and Sundays in Christianity. It wasn't until the late 1800s, during the Industrial Revolution, that the two-day weekend made an appearance as a response to the harsh conditions of factory work. Today, research indicates that a three-day weekend might prove even better in increasing productivity and boosting health and happiness.

Masculin

On the cool early days of Spring, the weekend is a time when it's better not to fight ennui, but embrace it.

Féminin

Photographs by Pelle Lannefors & Styling by Anna Klein

Previous page: Anine wears a top by Tibi and trousers by Filippa K. Linus wears a shirt by Issey Miyake.

Previous spread: Anine wears a top by Tibi and trousers by Dries Van Noten. Above: Linus wears a suit by Maison Margiela.

Anina wears a jacket and trousers by Yohji Yamamoto and shoes by Céline. Linus wears a shirt by Filippa K and trousers, shoes and hat by Yohji Yamamoto.

Left: Anine wears a top by Christian Wijnants, jacket by Koché, shorts by Christian Wijnants and shoes by Céline. Right: She wears a top and skirt by Prada.

Hair: Bénédicte Cazau Beyret, Makeup: Ania Grzeszczuk

Above: Anine wears a top by Lutz Huelle and trousers by Céline.

4

Directory

Silent through the height of her stardom in the 1960s and absent at the peak of her career, an enigmatic sculptor receives a renaissance in death.

SARAH MOROZ

Marisol Escobar

Although largely forgotten in recent decades, artist Marisol Escobar's public persona and creative output made a serious splash in the New York art world in the 1960s.

Operating on her own terms in a male-dominated scene, the French sculptor was "known for blithely shattering boundaries," as her obituary in *The New York Times* declared earlier this year. For one, Escobar maintained privacy in an age when the public thirsted for celebrity. She was described as "Garboesque" for her discretion: that is to say, on par with the famously reclusive habits of the Swedish-born actress. Escobar confounded others with her often-silent presence, but ultimately her shape-shifting ability was key to her success. "She can look like the stunning marquesa of a Fellini movie—or a beatnik kid on her way to a pot party," a contemporary once remarked of her.

Escobar's work addressed topics like kinship and womanhood with tongue in cheek, highlighting their inherent discomforts and absurdities. In *Love* (1962), an incomplete plaster face—nose to chin—is seen gulping back a glass bottle of Coca-Cola in an unnervingly evocative way. *The Family* (1962), painted on wooden planks, portrays a woman and her four children as little more than an awkwardly gathered group.

Escobar frequented the studio of Andy Warhol during the 1960s, and appeared in two of his experimental black-and-white films: *Kiss* (in which various couples kiss for three and a half minutes apiece; Escobar was paired with painter Harold Stevenson) and *13 Most Beautiful Women* (a compilation pulled from Warhol's wider series of screen tests).

In a 1965 *New York Times Magazine* profile—perhaps the most revealing press peek into her life—cultural reporter Grace Glueck showed Escobar to be self-assured and self-reliant. She transcended the insularity of underground film and art and attracted, as Glueck put it, "curiosity-seekers" to her exhibitions. "In this new American era of artist-as-star, she is asked to lecture by ladies' groups, gets letters from yearning teenagers and is recognized by businessmen in nightclubs," Glueck remarked.

Yet Escobar resisted the fame she garnered and often bolted from New York for several years at a time in favor of escapist travel. The scene shifted in her absence and she became less integral to it, inching further and further toward its fringes. Her more insinuating works of the 1960s would transform into blunt ferocity during the 1970s, evidenced by such titles as *I Hate You Creep and Your Fetus* (1973) and *Lick the Tire of My Bicycle* (1974).

When others accused Escobar of narcissism for her recurrent practice of integrating herself into her work, she countered: "The truth is, I use my own face because it's easier. When I want to make a face or hands for one of my pieces, I'm usually the only person around to use as a model." Her incorporation of her own anatomy was pragmatic, but also emphasized genuine ownership. Escobar noted, on carving her own path: "I don't feel you have to belong to a little group and then say everything not part of it is bad." Her career was hers, and she took it by the reins: "It has happened because I have made it happen," she said of being a professional artist. "I got tired of being a nobody... So I began to work very hard."

María Sol Escobar was born in Paris in 1930 to an affluent Venezuelan family. Her father was in real estate; her mother was an artist who committed suicide when Escobar was 11. Escobar grew up between Paris and Caracas until her family moved to Los Angeles in 1946. She returned to Paris to study at the École des Beaux-Arts, but it was a bad fit: "They wanted you to paint like Bonnard," she scoffed during the interview with Glueck. She signed up for courses at the Art Students League of New York instead, followed by classes at the New School for Social Research.

During this period, Escobar mingled regularly at the Cedar Tavern, which was then the Manhattan go-to for many abstract expressionists. She became friendly with several of them, notably Dutch-American action painter Willem de Kooning.

She rechristened herself Marisol when she began showing her work in New York in the late 1950s. Her first major solo exhibition was at the Leo Castelli Gallery—"the international epicenter for Pop, Minimal, and Conceptual Art"—in 1958. The year prior, she had been part of a pioneering group show alongside Jasper Johns and Robert Rauschenberg, and her work had already been shown at the Museum of Modern Art. Escobar's pop art sensibility merged with references to pre-Columbian artifacts; she constructed tableaux from assemblages of wood, plaster, terra cotta, textiles and found objects. "I do my research in the Yellow Pages," she told Glueck. "You could call them a new palette for me."

Humor, politics and pop culture were her principal thematic threads. *The Party*—an installation of blocky painted- and carved-wood figures ornamented with clothes, shoes and glasses—underlined both the artist's social malaise and the superficiality of the art scene. All of the 15 figures sported Escobar's visage, and none of them interacted with each other. Escobar's sculpture-portrait of Hugh Hefner, in which he is both smoking and holding a pipe, was featured on the March 3, 1967, cover of *Time* magazine ("The Pursuit of Hedonism," its banner blared). Like several of the identifiable figures she depicted, Hefner was as flattened as the lifestyle he represented.

A renewed interest in Escobar's work only came about in the waning years of her life: A 2014 solo show at the Memphis Brooks Museum of Art in Tennessee traveled to El Museo del Barrio in New York City. Her work resonates as authoritatively today as it ever did. The misrepresentation of women, the traumas of family, the hollowness of celebrity, the spectacle of the art industry: Escobar understood and articulated the shortcomings of the modern era.

Escobar, pictured in New York City in 1968, stands next to a seven-foot-tall bronze work titled *Father Damien*.

JARED KILLEEN

Imitation as Art

Touching countless readers with theories on love, language and literature, *Roland Barthes* turned his attention to an unlikely material: plastic.

Few materials withstand blows as well as plastic does. Its most eminent combatant, the meta-critic Roland Barthes, penned a famous essay in *Mythologies* denigrating the non-degradable product as "lost between the effusion of rubber and the flat hardness of metal." Yet what really bothered Barthes about plastic was not its cheapness or chemical complexion, but its lack of pretension. Unlike other synthetics—say, zirconium or laminate, which harbor ambitions of appearing expensive—plastic never pretends to be something it's not.

For Barthes, plastic also lacked an aesthetic: It is "hollow and flat," "engulfed in its usage." Yet plastic has outlived Barthes, as it has often done when confronted by the organic world. Today, it is the material as much as the man that enjoys renown in sophisticated urban circles. Witness the resurgence of 1950s design classics by Verner Panton and Charles and Ray Eames. Or the more recent work of Jasper Morrison and Ron Arad. By transfiguring the solemn and the frivolous, plastic embodies the most modern of aesthetics.

Left: In his collection of essays titled *Mythologies*, Barthes also meditates on the symbolic meanings of steak-frites, professional wrestling and Greta Garbo in *Queen Christina*.

Photograph: Joss McKinley, Styling: Yolande Gagnier

"Cynicism is actually the laziest stance you could take." What intelligent people still need to learn about the pursuit of wisdom.

DEBIKA RAY

Becoming Wise

In her book *Becoming Wise: An Inquiry into the Mystery and Art of Living*, broadcaster Krista Tippett collates insights from years of interviews from her award-winning radio show and podcast, *On Being*. Through dialogue with scientists, theologians, activists and poets, Tippett takes a broad view of the human condition—one more nuanced than that composed of facts and rationality alone.

Your book distills insights from your conversations with people from various walks of life. Why have you presented these under the banner of wisdom, rather than, say, knowledge? We've reached a moment where we've realized the limits of focusing on knowledge and rationality alone. We're more complicated than data can address and that has brought us back to the fact that in order to advance, we have to take the human condition seriously. Wisdom is one important way to talk about

the qualities we need to cultivate, to grapple with the complexities of this moment and rise to the best of our capacities. To me, the mark of a wise life is the imprint it makes on the world: The question of what it means to be human has become inextricable from the question of who we are to each other.

You mention listening and conversing as important components of attaining wisdom. Why is that? Because we need to cultivate a modicum of curiosity about the people we don't know or understand. We have allowed extreme voices to frame our most important public debates, but these don't represent almost all of us in between, who have some doubts or understand there's more we could know. What if we started to connect across our questions rather than our competing answers?

Is it easy to be cynical, given the state of public discourse? Cyni-

cism is actually the laziest stance you could take. If you choose it over hope, you don't have to lift a finger to make anything better. We have to let go of this instinct to fall into despair if politicians aren't doing something. It's a hard moment, because the places we traditionally looked to for answers are the most broken, but the upside is that this calls upon us to be citizens again—to start having the conversations we want to be hearing within our communities.

You close with a chapter on hope. Why do you distinguish this from optimism? Optimism has connotations of wishful thinking. Hope, to me, is robust and insists on a full picture of reality, which includes all the terrible things we read in the newspaper, but also takes seriously all the beautiful things around us, which are also part of the story of our time. I feel there's a hope muscle within us that we have to flex and make instinctive.

"The mark of a wise life is the imprint it makes on the world."

KRISTA TIPPETT

 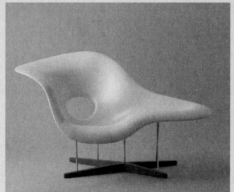 

LA CHAISE *by Molly Mandell*

While Charles and Ray Eames were not the first to design furniture using plastic, their work with the synthetic material has become some of the most celebrated. In 1948, just after World War II, the Museum of Modern Art in New York and the Museum Design Project, Inc., launched the Competition for Low-Cost Furniture. Intended to solve a lack of available low-priced furniture and improve post-war living standards, the contest drew 3,000 entries from around the world. It was here that the Eameses debuted their voluminous plastic design for La Chaise, its name and form both a nod to modernist sculptor Gaston Lachaise. Plastic was experiencing a coming of age—a synthetic novelty that, it seemed, could be used to make just about anything. Stamped steel and aluminum, the materials that the Eameses initially planned to use for La Chaise, had proved more difficult and expensive to produce than they had anticipated. In the end, the design duo did not walk away with a prize for La Chaise, but the chair garnered a great deal of attention and became almost immediately iconic. Yet La Chaise was not produced in the Eameses' lifetime: Even using plastic, it still cost too much to manufacture. Nearly 50 years later, in 1996, Vitra put the chair into production. Though designed to be low-cost, La Chaise has become an object of high value, a design classic and a much sought-after addition to many homes.

Photographs: Mikkel Mortensen

TOM MORRIS

Jonathan Anderson

Used to considering the human body in all of its forms, fashion designer *Jonathan Anderson* highlights disobedient ones as curator of a new exhibition.

BARBARA HEPWORTH
by Tom Morris

Barbara Hepworth was one of the leading lights of British modernism, practicing in a wide circle that included fellow sculptor Henry Moore (often referred to as a rival, when in fact they were chums and studied together) and painter Ben Nicholson, whom Hepworth married in 1938. She was born in the northern city of Wakefield in 1903 but took up residence in the southern coastal town of St. Ives during the Second World War. Her rounded, monumental sculptures— sculpted of wood, stone, bronze and clay—delved deeply, but abstractly, into the human form. Hepworth was a master at reducing form to a bare minimum combination of shapes, curves and planes. The parallels between her work and Jonathan Anderson's are subtle, but there. What Hepworth did with hard materials, Anderson has done with soft fabric: strange silhouettes and unpredictable structure. Where Hepworth hinted at the human form, however, Anderson often rewrites it entirely.

In 2015, Jonathan Anderson was awarded both womenswear and menswear designer of the year at the British Fashion Awards.

The Belfast-born fashion designer Jonathan Anderson—creative director both of his eponymous label J. W. Anderson and of Loewe—is known for his cross-cultural interests. This spring, he's curated the exhibition *Disobedient Bodies* at The Hepworth Wakefield, one of the UK's most important—and youngest—contemporary art centers. The exhibition explores the human form within sculpture, fashion and design, and includes works by Barbara Hepworth, Jean Arp, Louise Bourgeois and Lynn Chadwick, pitched alongside clothing by Christian Dior, Jean Paul Gaultier and Helmut Lang.

Which fashion designers have been particularly pioneering in exploring the human form? Issey Miyake is one of the most important people in fashion in the last hundred years. He revolutionized fashion with textiles, shape, form, technology and appropriation of art. Comme des Garçons is another fine example of that, as is Helmut Lang. These are all people whose work I think is as powerful as sculpture.

Where does the title of the show, "Disobedient Bodies," come from? It's about disobedience: When things don't conform, or you don't do as you're told, or the body or clothing doesn't react in the way you want it to.

Which sculptors do you cite as influences on the clothes you make? Barbara Hepworth was an incredible sculptor. Her approach, for its time, was extraordinarily important, though the significance of her work has only been widely acknowledged in the last 10 years. What she was doing was so sensitive, but she had this brutalist idea of the family, which she represented in a unique way. I also look to the work of Jean Arp, particularly how he was able to reduce a form.

What is their formal influence on your work? It's difficult to reinterpret sculpture into an actual fashion garment. A lot of things I draw are about the line or shape. When I think about heels, I think about someone like ceramic artist Hans Coper. I also love Sarah Lucas and her elongated shapes. We created a collection of men's knitwear with incredibly long sleeves, which was a formal exploration of how the body becomes elongated and disturbed.

What is the overall narrative of the exhibition? The exhibition sought out naturally occurring parallels in the worlds of fashion and sculpture: How someone like Jean Arp was exploring certain ideas, while Dior happened to be doing something similar at the same moment. How did these inter-connections happen? These days, we're so obsessed with what's done first, and what's not done first, and the idea of the show was to level everything out within fashion and sculpture.

How have you personally tried to investigate the human form? One of my objectives has been to explore the unisex wardrobe and what it means in terms of proportion, volume and shape. It stems from a collection I did that was based on ruffles on men, raising the question of how to challenge the shape of the male body. At the time, I was looking at very early Dior and how he played with a skirt length or volume that emphasized areas of the female body where volume wasn't ordinarily considered flattering. Over many, many years, it started to become diluted and become normalized. Men have not been challenged in quite the same way.

Disobedient Bodies: J.W. Anderson at The Hepworth Wakefield runs through June 18, 2017.

An artist's tip for falling short: Get back on the horse that threw you.

PIP USHER

Kentaro Yamada

"I'm often described as someone scared of jumping, metaphorically speaking," Kentaro Yamada says from Portugal, where he is busy visiting prehistoric cave paintings and admiring the ceramics of local artisans. Although he claims prudence, Kentaro's life—from competitive sailing to his career as an artist—doesn't appear hampered by cowardice or indecision. The trick, he claims, has always been to let his intuition lead the way. "Whenever I've achieved big steps or jumped to the next step, I didn't even know I was doing it," he concedes. "I was simply chasing my curiosity and my instinct. It's a good way for me to be."

As a teenager, instinct led Kentaro from Japan to New Zealand as he pursued dreams of sailing at the Olympics. But it was there that he experienced his first, jarring introduction to defeat. After he failed to perform as well as hoped at the World Championships, sporting ambition was relinquished in favor of creative pursuits. That led him to New York and Tokyo, back to New Zealand for a second degree and then on to Chicago for a master's in fine art. After a year of study, he burned out, overwhelmed by school's competitive nature and bogged down in a creative quagmire.

"It felt like a big failure when I quit my master's program at the School of the Art Institute of Chicago, where I had a scholarship," he remembers. "I moved to London thinking maybe this was the end of my artist's career, but after a while I realized that being an artist and being creative is not something I can escape. It's part of me, so I continued my master's at Goldsmiths."

With his work driven by a relentlessly inquisitive mind, art—be it ceramics, installation, film or sculpture—continues to be an integral part of Kentaro's DNA. "I'm interested in a long history—from the beginning of time to where we are now," he says of his propensity for probing some of life's colossal mysteries. "I think for most scientists and artists there's one big lingering question: Why the hell are we here, and how do we make sense of this world?"

Take his 2015 project, a dark, smoky perfume titled Neandertal, that utilized the unfamiliar terrain of scent to address questions about humanity's place in the universe. At face value, it's a $250 perfume designed with human origins in mind; scratch deeper, and Kentaro is poking holes at our human confidence in our singularity.

His enthusiasm for fragrance continued in a recent workshop at London's Victoria and Albert Museum titled Sound of Scent. Introducing participants to the centuries-old Japanese tradition of *kodo*, in which scent is said to be listened to rather than smelled, Kentaro encouraged them to mimic the classic poems that accompanied incense-burning by creating a narrative of their own. Blindfolded, the participants selected scents that represented their personal story and took home a bespoke fragrance at the workshop's end.

"With scent, it's very personal and goes directly to your memories and experiences," he explains. "It's a bit like a dream—the dream doesn't have to have a story, but it has an impact. There's a flash or experience that comes to you."

For Kentaro, constant existential scrutiny can come at a price. He admits to having had difficult periods, when the enormity of what he wanted to create, and his fear that he couldn't produce it, sank him into a sluggish state. But as he ages, a growing sense of perspective has left him better equipped for whenever those storm clouds hover threateningly overhead.

"If you realize this is just a phase, especially if you're asking some big existential question, then of course you will have these moments," he says. "I'm always trying to see things from the other side of life. If I looked back from my deathbed, what would I want to be doing? Art. That's how I'd probably be happy. That can give a good perspective on how to deal with everything."

Photograph: Mikkel Mortensen

MASTERING MISTAKES
by Molly Mandell

When jazz pianist Keith Jarrett arrived at the Cologne Opera House in 1975, he was greeted by a piano that was too small and poorly tuned. He nearly canceled the sold-out show but, after much desperate convincing from a young concert promoter, he performed. With an inadequate piano and a lot of frustration, Jarrett was forced to play differently that night. Concertgoers responded with zealous enthusiasm. Jarrett had turned a large mistake, albeit someone else's, into a masterpiece. "It's impossible to avoid mistakes," explains journalist and economist Tim Harford. "I suppose that you can try to avoid mistakes by never doing anything, but that would be a mistake in itself. It's much more practical to think about the ways we react to mistakes than to think about avoiding mistakes altogether." Both in conversation and in his new book, *Messy*, Harford suggests that obstacles and distractions can actually spur the most creative moments. "When pushed into the new and unfamiliar, two things happen," he says. "One is that you become tremendously alert. Either you or someone else has made a mistake, and now you have to fix it. Second, in the aftershock of encountering an obstacle, you may find yourself trying an otherwise unexpected solution." Harford encourages people to embrace their mistakes. "When you start from an unpromising beginning, you may find yourself at a much more interesting end point," he says. Jarrett certainly did: *The Köln Concert*, a live recording of his show, remains both the best selling solo jazz and solo piano album of all time.

Are you koalafied to answer this zoomorphic crossword? The search for animal monikers might drive you cuckoo.

MOLLY YOUNG

Crossword

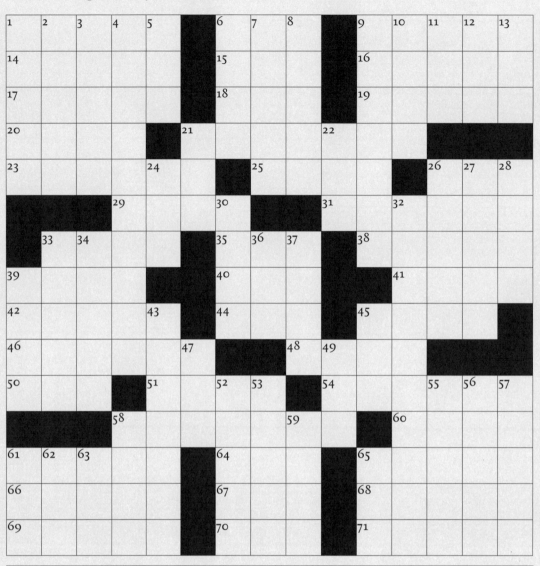

ACROSS

1. Stretch out your neck in order to see something
6. Bump hard against
9. Info on a bottle of whiskey or wine
14. Hiding, with "up"
15. Thurman of *Kill Bill*
16. Where to pin a pin
17. "Those girls," in Spanish
18. Steinbeck's *Of Mice and __*
19. Portal
20. Farm feed for pigs
21. Typographical glyph
23. Car company that originally manufactured looms
25. One kind of chef
26. Follow persistently
29. Island where the Venice Film Festival takes place
31. Birthplace of Jean-Jacques Rousseau
33. Misery
35. Hit at
38. The most expensive city in the Middle East
39. Formal agreement
40. Number of Top 40 hits performed by Steve Martin
41. Type of film or following
42. War story told in dactylic hexameter
44. Storm center
45. Data for mountains or airplane pilots, for short
46. Sport that can be played on clay, hard or grass courts
48. Back of the neck
50. Hoard without sharing
51. Fasten, as an envelope
54. Roams about for prey
58. High-pressure urbane life-style, colloquially
60. "Roof" in French
61. City official, in America
64. Blunder
65. Gender-bending Shakespeare character in *Twelfth Night*
66. Suffix with endo or proto-
67. "Give it ____!" ("Try it!")
68. Inklings
69. Rice wines
70. Plant seeds
71. Sit lightly

DOWN

1. Storage container for treasure
2. Viking who became the first ruler of Normandy
3. Metal mixture
4. Elena Ferrante's _____ *Novels*
5. Magazine staff, for short
6. 13th-century poet with widely translated works
7. Prayer endings
8. Fruit that inspired the first paisley patterns
9. Tickled
10. Diatribe
11. Choose
12. Literary preposition
13. Soar
21. Pops
22. Annoy
24. Cookie container
26. First performance
27. Some face shapes
28. Manner of walking
30. Woodwind
32. Genetic building block
33. Caveman-inspired dietary regimen
34. Breezing through
36. Whichever
37. Adolescent
39. Bitter part of citrus fruits
43. Renders harmless
45. Earth Day month, for short
47. Fix firmly in place
49. Mimic
52. Realms
53. Slow tempo
55. Romeo, for one
56. Flowering shrub with pale purple blooms
57. Tuck away in a safe place
58. Flower used for centuries in medicinal, culinary, and cosmetic applications
59. Boast unpleasantly
61. UK lawmakers
62. Pie ___ mode
63. Talk and talk and talk
65. A-lister

Margot Henderson

Kinfolk's contributing editor *Margot Henderson* cooks for between 30 and 200 people every day at her London restaurant, Rochelle Canteen. An influential chef, she's also a firebrand who manages to find small pleasures in peeling onions, the time to write cookbooks and enough energy to raise a family and still dance into the early hours.

Your usual breakfast: A flat white and Marmite on sourdough toast
The best compliment you've ever received: When Marina O'Loughlin reviewed Rochelle Canteen in The Observer, she wrote that my restaurant "wears its fabulousness lightly"
A meal you make when you eat alone: Miso and brown rice
A good book: Strange Weather in Tokyo by Hiromi Kawakami
A boring task that you secretly enjoy: Peeling onions
A comfort food: Pasta with tomato sauce
Your private refuge: My garden
An essential film: Marco Ferreri's La Grande Bouffe
A necessary fiction: That I'm a cab driver (I drive a black cab)
Values you've passed on to your children: To work hard and afterward, to sit around the table with friends and family and enjoy a good meal
A good habit of yours: I stay up late dancing
A bad habit: I stay up late dancing!

Stockists

ACNE STUDIOS
acnestudios.com

A DÉTACHER
adetacher.com

ALESSI
alessi.com

ANDREA JIAPEI LI
andreajiapeili.com

ANN-SOFIE BACK
annsofieback.com

BALENCIAGA
balenciaga.com

BASERANGE
baserange.net

BIALETTI
bialetti.com

CALVIN KLEIN
calvinklein.com

CÉLINE
celine.com

CHRISTIAN WIJNANTS
christianwijnants.com

CREATURES OF COMFORT
creaturesofcomfort.us

DKNY
dkny.com

DRIES VAN NOTEN
driesvannoten.com

EDUN
edun.com

FILIPPA K
filippa-k.com

FRAME
frame-store.com

HAY
hay.dk

HEIRS
heirs.at

HERMÈS
hermes.com

ICB
icbnyc.com

ISSEY MIYAKE
isseymiyake.com

JIL SANDER
jilsander.com

JOHN GALLIANO
johngalliano.com

JOSEPH
joseph-fashion.com

KALMAR
kalmarlighting.com

KOCHÉ
koche.fr

LOEWE
loewe.com

LUISAVIAROMA
luisaviaroma.com

LUTZ HUELLE
lutzhuelle.com

MAISON MARGIELA
maisonmargiela.com

MAISON NORDIK
maisonnordik.com

MALENE ODDERSHEDE BACH
maleneoddershedebach.com

MANSUR GAVRIEL
mansurgavriel.com

MARIA BLACK JEWELLERY
maria-black.com

MILLY
milly.com

MONSIEUR PARIS
monsieur-paris.com

MR. LARKIN
mrlarkin.net

PAUSTIAN
paustian.com

PILGRIM
pilgrim.dk

PRADA
prada.com

REJINA PYO
rejinapyo.com

ROBERTA EINER
robertaeiner.com

ROSA MOSA
rosamosa.com

SAGAN VIENNA
sagan-vienna.com

SAMUJI
samuji.com

SEA NEW YORK
sea-ny.com

SOPHIE BILLE BRAHE
sophiebillebrahe.com

STUDIO NICHOLSON
studionicholson.com

STUTTERHEIM
stutterheim.com

TAKEHOMEDESIGN
takehomedesign.com

TIBI
tibi.com

TOPMAN
topman.com

URIBE
studiouribe.co.uk

VITRA
vitra.com

VITSØ
vitsoe.com

WÄSTBERG
wastberg.com

WORKSTEAD
workstead.com

WRKDEPT
wrkdept.com

YOHJI YAMAMOTO
yohjiyamamoto.co.jp

tf

ISSUE 23

Credits

COVER
Photograph
Stefan Heinrichs

Styling
Rose Forde

P.25
Hair and Makeup
Carly Lim
Top by *Rejina Pyo*

P.30 — 31
Products
Time Hourglasses by Hay

P.32 — 33
Hair and Makeup
Yasmina Bentaieb

P.32
Top by *Malene Oddershede Bach*, suit by *Roberta Einer* and jewelry by *Pilgrim*

P.33
Sweater by *Rejina Pyo*, trousers by *Roberta Einer*, earcuff by *Maria Black* and rings by *uRibe* and *Pilgrim*

P.38
Location
Casa Renacimiento in Atotonilco, Mexico

P.45
Shirt by *Calvin Klein*

P.46
Shirt by *Zara*

P.48 — 61
Hair
Paul Donovan

Makeup
Naoko Scintu

Photography Assistants
Simon Wellington
Jacob Muller Meernach

P.66 — 77
Makeup
Steffie Lamm-Siu

P.78 — 91
Images courtesy of
Dance Theatre of Harlem

P.93
Location
Pomellato, Milan

P.100 — 102
Location
Hôtel Saint-Marc

P.103
Location
Casa Fayette

P.104
Location
Dimore Gallery

P.114 — 127
Hair
David Cruz

Makeup
Bryan Zaragoza

Photography Assistant
Donna Viering

Styling Assistant
Danielle Terry

P.138 — 145
Artworks from series Chicago, 1988 (images on p. 139 and 142 are details)

P. 168 — 176
Hair
Bénédicte Cazau-Beyret

Makeup
Ania Grzeszczuk

Model
Anine Van Velzen at IMG

Model
Linus Wordemann at Success

Photography Assistant
Andreas Sönnergren

Styling Assistant
Rebecka Häggblom

Styling Assistant
Dominyka Angelyte

Products
Chairs from Maison Nordik

P.181
Products
Eames La Chaise courtesy of Paustian

P.182
Photograph courtesy of *the Witt Library, The Courtauld Institute of Art, London*

SPECIAL THANKS
Brooke McClelland
John Shegda
Theara Ward
Anna Glass
Stephen Daiter Gallery
Craig B. Highberger
Bureau de Marc Riboud
Irene Houstrup
Zachary Adrian Combs